BALLANTINE BOOKS
NEW YORK

JEFFREY MOUSSAIEFF MASSON

✽

RAISING
THE PEACEABLE
KINGDOM

✽

What Animals Can Teach Us About the Social
Origins of Tolerance and Friendship

Published in the United States by Ballantine Books, an imprint of The Random House Publishing Group, a division of Random House, Inc., New York.

BALLANTINE and colophon are registered trademarks of Random House, Inc.

Library of Congress Cataloging-in-Publication Data

Masson, J. Moussaieff (Jeffrey Moussaieff)
Raising the peaceable kingdom : what animals can teach us about the social origins of tolerance and friendship / Jeffrey Moussaieff Masson.
p. cm.
ISBN 0-345-46613-6 (alk. paper)
1. Social behavior in animals.   2. Toleration.   3. Animal psychology.   I. Title.

QL775.M37 2005
591.5'1—dc22   2005048210

Printed in the United States of America on acid-free paper

www.ballantinebooks.com

2 4 6 8 9 7 5 3 1

First Edition

Text design by Caroline Cunningham

For Leila

Contents

Introduction: An Experiment About
Peaceful Coexistence   3

One: Starting the Peaceable Kingdom   11

Two: Reality Sets In (Trouble in Paradise)   51

Three: The Peaceable Kingdom   97

Four: Transformations   115

Five: All Good Things Must End   143

Epilogue: Applying the Results to Humans   155

Acknowledgments   169

RAISING
THE PEACEABLE
KINGDOM

Introduction:
An Experiment About Peaceful
Coexistence

THIS BOOK IS about a simple, benign experiment, or perhaps we should call it an inquiry, to learn what are the essential ingredients in interspecies friendships and even love. The basic idea was to raise together a kitten, a puppy, a bunny, a chick, and a baby rat in close circumstances to see if they would all get along and even become good friends.

A modest enough venture, and not only one that I hoped would be successful, but—considering the religious hatred, bigotry, war, and political animosity that appear on the front pages of our newspapers every day—one that I hoped in the end might offer some lessons to us humans, lessons that we might apply to the sorry state of our own relationships with one another.

I deliberately set out to achieve what usually happens only accidentally. What I wanted to know was whether animals who normally do not associate could, if raised together from an early age, learn to overcome a tendency toward at best indifference, and at worst enmity, and learn to tolerate one another, perhaps even play, develop friendship, and, with luck, become soul mates. There are many reports of this happening accidentally, but I have not heard of a concerted attempt to observe the process from beginning to end. In any event, what did I have to lose? I hoped to adopt animals whose prospects were not otherwise good. Even if my project failed, at least I would have given all of these animals a happier and a freer life than they would have been likely to have otherwise.

There is no doubt that tolerance can be learned. After all, tolerance is not an emotion. Even though we can say, colloquially, that we are "feeling tolerant," what we really mean is that we have made a conscious decision about something that demands us to think. Tolerance is a point of view, and points of view can be learned, they can be taught to others and transmitted via acts and words. Affection, on the other hand, is different. You cannot coerce affection, you cannot force one animal to like or love another animal. But the *conditions* that permit affection to grow can be cultivated, encouraged, and rewarded.

That is what I set out to do. I hoped, first of all, that the animals would cease to consider one another as enemies or to feel threatened. Second, I wanted them to tolerate one another. I hoped tolerance would lead to conditions that made playing together possible. Playing together would lead or could lead to friendship. Finally, it was my perhaps unrealistic hope that an animal might discover his or her soul mate in an animal from a different species. In my own experience, I had seen all but the last. (Tolerating an animal, becoming friendly with an animal, and feeling you have found your soul mate are all different conditions; a close friend, as opposed to a soul mate, is still not somebody you are inseparable from.) I had known dogs to become close friends with cats, and I had even seen some cats, if their training was begun early enough, bond with a bird. This was not surprising, but there *was* surprisingly little written about it beyond the anecdotes themselves, of which there are hundreds, if not thousands. I may not be the first to ask these questions, or even the first person to conduct this very experiment, but I may be the first person to write it up at any length.

At least half the reason I began this project (a less disturbing word for some than *experiment*) was to see if I could, in this manner, learn more about the essential characteristics of enmity between human groups and, by extension, what made for the opposite—comity, friendship, cooperation, affection, empathy, and even compassion. Almost every explanation that has been proposed in the past has been shown to be lacking, beginning with the most supposedly cohesive of all bonds, that of blood ties (family). Family ties do not guarantee cooperation, empathy, compassion, or even love. We have only to remember Tolstoy's famous opening lines of his novel *Anna Karenina*: "Happy families are all alike; every unhappy family is unhappy in its own way"—hence interesting (at least to the novelist). But it is not only fiction; unhappiness within families has spawned a whole genre of memoirs in recent years.

Language: People who speak the same language are nonetheless often at one another's throats (witness the natives of Bangladesh and India, or Irish Catholics and Irish Protestants, or Serbs and Croats). Religion: Internecine strife *between* religions is so common that it almost feels *normative.* Think of Israel and the Palestinians; Indian strife between Muslims and Hindus; Bosnian Muslims and Serbians from the Orthodox Church; the murderous hatred in Chechnya between Russian Orthodox Christians and Muslims; Sri Lanka, where the Buddhists and Hindus are eager to kill one another; East Timor, where the killing is between Christians and Muslims. Even within religions there is animosity: Look at the "troubles" in Northern Ireland between Catholics and Protestants, or think of the Sunni and Shiite differences in Pakistan and other countries in the Middle East. Race: Hatred of white toward white (Europe) and black toward black (Africa) is, alas, all too common and has always been so. Nationality is often used as an exclusionary tool (as in the Third Reich). In France today, a common nationality (that is, citizenship) is not sufficient to create harmony between Muslims living in impoverished housing developments on the outskirts of Paris and other Parisians. The Balkans has given us the term *balkanization* to refer to internal turmoil and schisms of all kinds. Hardly any modern country is without some form of this dreaded condition. Class: Political groups cross class lines and are perfectly capable of expressing disdain and even going to war with one another. Dress, habits, and cultural similarities may help us choose friends, or even mates, but they do not prevent internecine struggle.

Are we bound, then, to hate outsiders? Is there a sociobiology of ethnocentrism that declares an in-group and an out-group a genetic heritage that we are doomed to repeat endlessly? Does science provide us with no way out? If we can take no comfort in recent history, is there any reason to believe humans capable of developing the necessary feelings or the necessary intelligence or the necessary information that makes tolerance and goodwill possible?

I am hardly the first to note the interesting fact that no scientist speaks of enmity among animals of different species. Animals may hunt one another and eat one another, but the word *hatred* would seem out of place for any of them. The cat does not hate the mouse; he simply eats the mouse. He does not think "enemy"; he thinks "dinner." Even when the cat looks askance at another cat, it is not hatred; it is not about not being like him, it is about territory or rivalry for reproductive success. The cat does not need to construct elaborate and purely imaginative categories into which to place different animals to justify his actions.

Moreover, most animals do not have conflicts with other animals in the wild. They seem to ignore one another except when they have no choice. How did they achieve this? When forced together, animals do much better than we do. That is what gave me the idea for this book: If animals from different species not known for their friendship can learn to tolerate one another and perhaps go even further than tolerance, why could we not do the same?

How artificial is it to create the conditions that may lead to a "peaceable kingdom"? Well, we should remember that *all* animals living with humans live in artificial conditions. Except, perhaps, for the cat, no animal has *chosen* to live with humans without coercion, whether as a pet, in a zoo, in a circus, or on a farm.

The ideal, of course, would be to observe animals in the wild over a period of many years. This is what all the great ethologists of our time have done, and with great success: Dian Fossey, Biruté Galdikas, Jane Goodall, Cynthia Moss, Joyce Poole, and many others. But their writings contain virtually no observations of interspecies friendship, not because these sensitive observers are unwilling to describe them, but because the circumstances under which animals in the wild make friends across the species barrier are very rare.

———

THE IDEA OF a peaceable kingdom is attractive because it speaks to a deep hunger many of us have to live in harmony and peace with one another and with members of other species, even though we know that our history does not suggest this is possible. How to achieve that goal is possibly the single most important question anyone can ask. Finding the solution or the direction of the solution is hardly a trivial pursuit. Who would ever say: My goal is to create conflict, anger, and ultimately war? Nobody.

Yet we must not lose our humility over our historic inability to understand the feelings of other people, let alone members of other species. We need to remember that one of the greatest minds of the Western world (Aristotle) thought that slavery was natural, that there were *born* slaves just as nineteenth-century psychiatrists believed (and many still do) that there are *born* criminals. Most people no longer hold such benighted views. Which of our current cherished ideas will appear inane in the future?

One thousand years from now, we will almost certainly look back with horror and incredulity at many of our beliefs and practices. A bit of humility among scientists is always a good thing. I fully expect that future humans will find it hard to believe that zoos, circuses, and factory farms ever existed. But I could be wrong. For thousands of years, our behavior toward animals did not improve greatly. Only in the last twenty or thirty years has our attitude begun to change.

What we can be certain of, though, is that our knowledge of animals will expand enormously, particularly our knowledge of their thoughts and feelings. These are the very areas that have been most neglected by animal scientists until quite recently. Part of the reason has been that we have not had occasion to live on terms of intimacy with animals. You cannot understand the inner life of a rat if your acquaintance with the rat is confined to laboratories. Your child who has a pet rat is likely to know more than you do about the feelings of the rat and even about the rat's behavior. Did any of the thousands of scientists who observed rats or pigeons in laboratories leave us with any convincing accounts of their inner lives? If so, I have missed them. It is like hunters: Almost no knowledge about elephant behavior comes from elephant hunters. In fact, I will go further: We learned *nothing* about the lives of elephants from the books of elephant hunters. Only when women went into the field and simply watched elephant families did our knowledge begin to grow.

It is only once we have made the decision to live with an animal on some sort of equal ground that we are likely to learn what that animal is capable of from a more complex point of view: not just what they do during any given day, what they eat, and how they mate, but also how they find joy, what makes them sad, how they grieve, and even how they might express compassion for a companion or a friend. My experiment was an attempt to imitate as far as possible a natural experiment; to learn some of the lessons of field observations. It is not meant to resemble a laboratory experiment. And perhaps these animals will have something to teach us, too.

ONE

⊶⊰⊱⊷

STARTING THE PEACEABLE
KINGDOM

ONCE I HAD MADE the decision to try to create a peaceable kingdom, my first challenge was to make sure all five species entered our home as close to the same moment as possible. I didn't want territoriality to be a factor in how the animals related to one another. The more quickly I could find all the right baby animals, the more successful the bonding process was likely to be, with one another and with us. I did not want one animal to be there weeks before another and to claim territory or seniority. I wanted the playing field to be more or less level. Speed was therefore of the essence. I had to get a puppy, a kitten, a chick, a bunny, and a baby rat within as short a time period as possible.

From where should I get them? Ideally, I wished to rescue animals who needed a home, not purchase them. The principle was that if I could guarantee a "good" life to animals who would otherwise have a not-so-good life, my taking the animals into my home could be justified. We don't want animals bred when there are many waiting for a home. Each animal bought is one fewer animal adopted.

In America, this would undoubtedly have been easy to achieve. For every species there is a group of dedicated people who rescue its animals from abusive situations. Indeed, for dogs there is a rescue group for each and every breed.

There are people devoted to rescuing cats, rabbits, and chickens and expanding public awareness of what wonderful companions these animals can make. You do not need to buy any of these animals in the United States and should never do so without compelling reasons.

In New Zealand, however, such rescue groups do not yet exist. Perhaps it is simply too small a country. For example, in New Zealand there are no farm sanctuaries where rescued animals can live out their lives free of the prospect of being killed for food, whereas such places are becoming more common in the United States, in Canada, and in Great Britain (I list many of them at the end of my book *The Pig Who Sang to the Moon*). Nor was there a group that could help me rescue a rat or a rabbit from a laboratory and its perhaps cruel, pointless, or unethical experiments.

But in New Zealand we do have the Society for the Prevention of Cruelty to Animals (SPCA), and from them you can adopt dogs and cats and sometimes other animals. So one sunny, cloudless Saturday in January, our whole family—my wife, Leila, and our sons, Ilan, seven, and Manu, two—drove to their adoption center near the airport in Auckland. I told the director, Bob Kerridge, what I was looking for and why. They could find me a dog and a cat, he told me. As for the rats, we were lucky, because just that day two had come in.

"Here, have a look," the woman behind the counter told us, and pulled out two seven-week-old hooded domestic rats.* They were mostly white but had what looked like dark brown hoods over their faces—a naturally occurring fur color that humans select because it is considered attractive. "They are in dire need of a home. Rats are still not that popular here, and unless we find them a home soon, they will have to be euthanized."

Ilan was enchanted with them and needless to say appalled at the fate that might well await them. "They are so cute! Look at their little fingernails," he said. Sure enough, their tiny paws had delicate, shiny fingernails. Children immediately notice how much like us even a rat is, whereas adults focus on the "yuck" factor. (See page 14 for a photo of Rebecca with Kia on her shoulder and Moana in her arms.) Leila, for example, noticed their long, snakelike tails. One of the rats hopped onto Ilan's shoulder, and he has not wished to be separated from her since. We decided to name them Kia and Ora (*kiore* is the Maori

---

*The domestic rat is descended from *Rattus norvegicus,* the scientific term for the wild rat, who looks identical to the domestic rat. Indeed, they are hardly a different species and will certainly interbreed. The only real difference is temperament. One is tame, the other "savage," or so we believe.

word for "rat," and *Kia ora* is the Maori greeting). I was a bit worried at the prospect of having an endless number of rat pups if they were male and female (who, after all, would take them?) but was assured they were two sisters.

"As for a puppy, come out the back, and we will bring you several eight-week-old puppies that are now here and you can see if you like one."

We had actually brought with us a dog psychologist, a

Dutchman by the name of Flip, who had volunteered to do a "personality test" on the puppies to see which one would fit in best with our household. I was not keen on the idea, because I have a distrust of tests in general and especially psychological tests. In my psychoanalytic training, I had to learn a bit about diagnostic tests for people, and I always abominated them. How could you find out about the inner life of a person by giving a test? It seemed absurd, and the more I learned, the less I liked them.

Still, I had to admit that all three puppies brought to us seemed perfect, and I would have had a difficult time choosing. So I let Flip do his test. He selected one of the three puppies, a mixture of blue heeler and German shorthaired pointer, because he said she was remarkably docile and submissive. For my "experiment," I did not want a difficult, aggressive dog eager to prove her place at the top of the hierarchy. This dog did not fight for food, and she came when called. She was curious and alert and friendly. He put her on her back and held her down gently but firmly to see how much she would struggle. Ideally, she would protest briefly, then submit. She passed the test. I did not think too deeply about the theories behind the test; they are widely used and probably have some validity, though I remain skeptical. Still, I had no better way of selecting one of the three and asked for a week to think it over. There were two other puppies, both golden retrievers, for which I have always had affection, and although they did not "test" as well, they were adorable, and making such a momentous decision seemed almost impossible. I would have liked to get a kitten at the SPCA, too, and begin my project with all the animals at once, but no kittens were available.

When we got home, I made my first mistake: I introduced the rats to Megala, my three-year-old Bengal cat, who immediately scared them into a small box we had placed in their (temporary) cage in our living room as a little hideaway. (You can see their initial encounter in the photo on page 17.) It was a few hours before they would come out again. How naive of me to think that just because *I* believed the rats were safe, they should trust me. Trust me? Why should they trust me when they didn't know me? In any event, what did I really know about Megala's tolerance for a pet rat? Impatience is one of my worst traits: I wanted the project to be in full bloom before it had even started—and in any event, introducing the rats to my three-year-old cat was not even part of the project.

I also needed to find a chicken, and here the SPCA could be of no help. People rarely brought in chickens for rehoming. I called around and spoke to a few hatcheries. Could I come when a chick was being hatched and take the chick home that day? Sure, I was told. Fortunately, I found an expert at the university who warned me of the dangers in this: Chicks need their mother for at least seven weeks, just like kittens and puppies. They need to be kept warm at night; they need to learn what and how to eat, what to be afraid of and what not to be afraid of; they need to hear reassuring clucks that no human can imitate with complete success. In short, they had to learn to be

chickens, and the best way to be taught that was by their mother, not me. It made perfect sense.

A few days later, I was given a tip about a man, George Hogan, who lives on the outskirts of Auckland with hundreds of birds in his backyard, including parrots, doves, and chickens of all breeds. Our whole family drove out to see him and his birds.

"Why," I asked him, "do you have so many chickens?"

"I don't know," he answered, "but I have always loved birds and can never remember a time when I did not have many."

I told him about my project, and he found the idea appealing. He showed me his favorite chickens: Polish frizzles. There are all kinds of "frizzles," a word that refers to the kind of feathers the chicken has. They stick up and make the chickens look as though they have just come back from a fancy hairdressing salon. He offered me a pair of seven-week-old siblings. "Never get a single chicken—it will pine away from loneliness. Chickens are sociable—they need company." (This was a vast understatement, I was later to learn.)

"Are they both hens, or is one a rooster?" I asked.

He corrected me. "The proper term for a young male is a cockerel. When they are older, they are called roosters or cocks. The young female is called a pullet and becomes a hen only later." Chicken, it turns out, is the generic name. "Chickens are very hard to sex," he admitted. "I'm not sure what you have here." He thought I might have one of each, but he could not really say, except to tell me this: "Your neighbors will know soon enough, if one starts crowing at four a.m. My neighbors don't mind," he told me. "Yours might not, either." (Oh, so wrong.) I was not exactly worried about having a male and a female and therefore baby chicks. I thought our whole family would find the idea of watching eggs hatch enchanting.

I liked the idea of having a crowing rooster. Nobody seems to know why roosters crow when they do, and I was eager to find out.

We put the two young chickens in a cat-carrying box (useful for rabbits and rats, too, as we discovered) and began the half-hour drive back to our beach house. Both Manu and Ilan were wildly excited. Suddenly it struck me that I was now in charge of the lives—let me repeat that, the *lives*—of two completely unknown beings. What if I failed them? There seemed so much I needed to know about them, so much to learn, and I was so ignorant. I felt like a first-time father coming home from the hospital with a baby and a completely blank mind. There was no Dr. Spock for chickens, only poultry manuals, and how could I possibly trust them, each one of which had a chapter on butchering?

As soon as I got home I put the chickens, whom we decided to call Moa (the Maori word for a large extinct flightless bird that looked like a large ostrich) and Moana (the Maori word for "ocean," but it also sounds like the feminine of Moa) in a large aviary I had had built for them out of wood and mesh. A dozen wild birds could have lived there comfortably, but it was even better for two small chickens. I don't call it a cage because it is so large and is in the enclosure—a large courtyard with chicken wire over the top and no way for any predator to get inside— behind our house. (See the photo on page 20 of me, Hohepa, and Mika in the enclosure.)

Once they were in the aviary, they were quiet for an hour. Then they started calling. I went out and spoke with them and whistled, imitating bird sounds, and that seemed to calm them. So I left. Then they started calling again. I went back. They stopped. It was now nine p.m., and I discerned the pattern. They called, I came. I was right to be apprehensive. This was, after all, not just *like* an adoption, it *was* an adoption. On my last trip, two of my older cats, Megala and Moko, slipped

into the courtyard where the aviary was. The chickens seemed unfazed. Had they ever seen a cat? I decided to ask their previous owner. (I can't bring myself to call him a companion, because he eats chicken, though never his own, he explained to me. Yes, they had seen cats, he told me.) The cats were mesmerized. The chickens were so close, yet so unattainable inside their comfortable but transparent cage. As the chickens grew, would these two grown cats come to accept them as family? Stay tuned.

I was eager to see if one of them, or both, would crow. A rooster doesn't normally crow until he is about five months old. At first there is an odd little noise that comes out, then finally a proper crow. They can do this, though, only if they have heard other roosters crow. Mine had, though by the time he would have the vocal capacity to crow, his memory of having heard older roosters crow would be months behind him. Would that matter? Would he make an odd and eccentric crow of his own?

Of course, I wasn't even certain whether one or both of the chickens was male. It is strange to think that the sexing of chickens is a difficult art, but it is. Here in New Zealand, a tester sets up at a table and checks each chick (by looking up his or her rear end—it is called "cloacal testing" and was invented by two Japanese scientists in 1934; until then, you simply had to wait until behavior showed you the difference), which either passes or fails the test. (In the United States, color sexing is used; chickens are bred so that males are predominantly white and females brown.) Since the point of these chickens' existence is to lay eggs, the tragedy (there is no more appropriate word) is that if the chicken is a male, he is immediately killed, either by suffocation or, even more horribly, by being thrown alive into a shredder.

NEXT I NEEDED to find a cat. Our household already had five adult cats, all of whom hunted birds, mice, rats, lizards, and praying mantises. I have never been comfortable with this, even though I felt the cats did not have much of a choice—they evolved to be hunters, and it was not their fault that they had been introduced into New Zealand. My neighbors, many of whom are especially fond of New Zealand native birds, have been even less comfortable with their hunting than I was. I was aware, however, of a certain hypocrisy in my neighbors, who loved birds but ate one particular bird, the chicken, without giving it a thought. After all, the average human meat eater will consume about three thousand chickens in the course of his or her life; the average cat kills a much smaller number of birds over his or her life.

I wanted to find a kitten for the project, but my neighbors did not want me to introduce yet another predator into our little paradise down at the beach. I agreed with them. Neither Leila nor I wanted to open our home to one more carnivore, one more animal who would hunt without compunction. (And who expects cats to display compunction?) As vegetarians, we did not want to have to buy meat for one more animal.

The only solution was to find a cat who did not hunt. I knew of only one breed of cat well known for their indifference, even aversion, to hunting and for being so docile that it does not occur to them to hurt another animal: the rag doll. Unfortunately, the only way to acquire such a cat is through a breeder. Normally, as I have already said (and one cannot say this often enough), I oppose the idea of breeding animals for pleasure or for profit. But in deference to my neighbors and to our own preferences and inclinations, we gave in and bought a rag doll kitten from a breeder. So came the mighty Tamaiti (Maori for "child") into our life. And even though I was buying rather than rescuing this particular cat, I knew that he would have a life of freedom on our beach, one unlikely to be duplicated anywhere else. So to

some extent I may have been rescuing him from a less rewarding life. Or so I tell myself. Perhaps I just need to salve my con-
science a bit here.

The dog and the cat were one thing: I *knew* dogs and cats. I
had lived with both animals all of my childhood and a good part
of my adult life. But rats and chickens? What did I really know
about them? I had lived with hamsters and gerbils as a child,
but rats were a different species, even if they resembled their
smaller cousins physically. I could not pretend to knowledge I
did not possess. Sure, I had learned certain basics from books—
for example, that rats greet you by yawning—but a manual
cannot replace experience. After eight years of psychoanalytic
training, I realized that there are no experts when it comes
to human emotion. It is not a subject you can learn in a class or
from a manual the way you can learn about car mechanics or
even about the functions of the human body. Leila is a pediatrician, and she has come to the same conclusion about raising
children. Reading books and seeing children in the hospital was
one thing, but until she had her own, it was only theory. Why
should it be any different for animals? This has great implications for all of us: Every time we take an animal into our life, we
have an opportunity to be creative and even to make basic dis-
coveries. Think of Dr. Irene Pepperberg and Alex, the gray par-
rot who knows the meaning of several hundred words; or Mark
Bekoff and his discovery of the grammar of the play bow among
dogs; or Donald Griffin and his discovery of bat sonar. Cats still
retain their basic mystery, and in spite of some five thousand

books written about our feline companions, nobody has yet cracked the code. So much remains to be discovered.

I thought I knew rabbits because I had lived with many rabbits, both as a child and as an adult. But in fact I did not know rabbits. An example of my ignorance: I didn't know whether it would be better to have one rabbit or two living with us. Are rabbits solitary, as many animal behavior scientists claim, or are they sociable, as the devotees of the House Rabbit Society (a group of passionate domestic-rabbit aficionados) claim? I am still not sure. A rabbit who lives in a house is, after all, not an outdoor rabbit. Would my rabbit want a hole to live in, or would he be happy in a house that was safe for him? Would he want to feel grass under his feet, or would he be indifferent to such matters? What would he want to eat? I didn't want to feed him just pellets or pet-store-bought rabbit food. Would he like or fear the dog, the cat, the chickens, and the rats? It was all a mystery to me.

As I mentioned earlier, I would have preferred to come by a rabbit by liberating one from a laboratory where unnecessary and abominable experiments are performed to determine whether floor polish and other essentials of life are safe for humans to use. The method, called "draize testing," is used to see how many rabbits go blind or die from having the compounds poured into their sensitive eyes. I could not count on any assistance, however, for such a plan. As far as I know, nobody in New Zealand rescues rabbits from labs. I would have had to do it on my own, and it would have meant breaking the law. I have no problem with people who break into facilities to rescue animals living in pure misery, but I don't think I could do it myself. Moreover, I needed a bunny large enough to withstand the attentions of the kitten and the puppy and my older cats. I had had many rabbits in my life,* and I knew for certain that each was an individual. I had known rabbits who were docile, friendly, and easygoing. Others seemed almost malevolent, intent on biting and terrorizing the household. One large white male rabbit chased my cats mercilessly from room to room, with amorous intentions they found repugnant. He did not understand the meaning of no.

A Flemish giant was the way to go, the Auckland Zoo assured me. They had them in the children's petting zoo and found them very sociable with other species. That was half my battle, so I asked for the phone number of the local breeder. When I went there, I found that although I was "buying" a rabbit (for a nominal fee), I was also liberating him from a life confined to a small cage in a smelly basement. It was immediately clear that just about anything would improve the life he was destined to live here (for what purpose did not invite scrutiny). So it was that Hohepa (Maori for "Joseph"—it is not that I felt anything special for the name Joseph, but I love the sound of Hohepa) came into our lives a few days after the chickens. He

---

*See my foreword to the most complete book about rabbits I know: *Stories Rabbits Tell: A Natural and Cultural History of a Misunderstood Creature* by Susan E. Davis and Margo Demello, foreword by Jeffrey Moussaieff Masson. N.Y.: Lantern Books, 2003.

had just been weaned at about seven weeks and was ready to be on his own. I was all for keeping him together with one of his siblings, but the man who raised him said rabbits preferred to live by themselves. He was not terribly convincing, but he did seem to know more about rabbits than I did. (Below you can see a photo of Moana thoroughly investigating a puzzled-looking rabbit.)

I think Hohepa must have been in a state of shock the day we brought him home. I had never seen a more docile, compliant animal. The next day, however, we could hardly catch him. This reminds of me of an experience I had years ago while living in Calcutta, India. A man came to my room in the Ramakrishna Vedanta Center with a tiny chipmunk he was eager to sell for what seemed then like an astronomical fee. He justified the fee

with a remarkable spiel: "This is the tamest wild chipmunk I have ever known; he adores people and just likes staying in your hand. There has never been another like him. He is worth his weight in gold." I succumbed, and it is true that the chipmunk was remarkably tame—for the entire time the drug was still working, that is. It was obvious that he had been drugged, sedated, or medicated, because the next day he was so wild that I had to release him. Well, Hohepa's drug was fear. Strange, though, how kittens never go through this stage. (An adult cat, however, will often hide under a bed for days when moved to a new environment; cats loathe change.) Is that the difference between a carnivore and a prey animal? Fear just seems built into the genes of the vulnerable rabbit, whereas Tamaiti the kitten carried himself with the confidence of the ultimate predator.

WHEW—SUDDENLY WE WERE peopling our lives with lots of animals! Only the dog was missing. So back to the SPCA we went, to revisit the three puppies. We decided to trust Flip and his personality test and take the blue heeler/German shorthaired pointer mix. She had been found wandering the streets of Manurewa in South Auckland as a puppy, picked up as a stray by Animal Control, and slated to be euthanized when the SPCA decided to take her in and give her a chance to be adopted. She was about eleven or twelve weeks old. Young enough, I thought then, to be completely trainable. Now, however, I believe that a lot can happen to a puppy in the first eleven weeks of life that may not be so easy to overcome. I think this puppy must have had some unhappy experiences in those early weeks that left her with character traits not easy to erase.

We called her Mika, a good Maori name, and at last we knew our family was complete. The dog trainer Flip and I immediately began a good-natured argument about training. I was for less, he was for more. However, we both agreed that for the sake of the dog's own safety, as well as for the convenience of the humans with whom the dog lives, she needed to know commands such as "stay" and "leave it." It was a question not of tricks, but of life and death. "Stay" could save the life of a dog who was heading into traffic unaware of the danger. While I still maintain that Elizabeth Marshall Thomas's book *The Hidden Life of Dogs* is the best book about dogs I know, I would not want to repeat her experiment of allowing a dog to wander freely in a city like Cambridge, Massachusetts.

Flip uses the clicker method (working with a metal clicker and rewarding with food to reinforce the connection between the click and the target behavior every time the dog does what you want) pioneered by Karen Pryor, and he came down to the beach to demonstrate. I was skeptical at first but was soon convinced that it works, even though I prefer the human voice and the warmth of praise rather than treats. Using food seemed like cheating to me, but Flip thought I was being overly sentimental, and he may have had a point. I must admit that the training went faster with food treats, and rewarding an animal does not have to mean going back to the bad old days when they were punished as well. And after all, we wanted Mika to have good puppy manners as soon as possible: We didn't want her jumping up on people when they arrived, refusing to come when we called her, or picking up yucky things on the beach (I still remember the command "leave it" from the three dogs I lived with in Berkeley from 1995 to 1998 and how much I liked using it and being listened to; it is a most useful phrase for a dog to learn).

We did not even *attempt* clicker training on Tamaiti the kitten, of course. "Stay!" "Leave it!" "Come now!" How absurd these commands are when aimed at a cat. I know, for I have tried them out. All I got for my efforts were a yawn and a contemptuous glance back as he walked slowly out of the room. You cannot exercise control over a cat. This is one of the many reasons that men—who like to be obeyed—generally prefer dogs to cats. It is amazing how quickly Tamaiti has adapted to the household, however. He has the run of the house (and the outdoors) now, but true to his breed, he rarely strays far from the front of our property, though he does walk down to the beach with us.

I REMEMBER HOW I was almost driven to despair when three dogs joined our household in one week so that I could begin research for my book *Dogs Never Lie About Love*, about the emotional world of dogs. It was like suddenly having three children in my life. There was the work, the responsibility, and the fear of failure. For a week I went into something like a depression. I did not think I could handle it. Well, I had something of the same reaction again now that all the animals (seven of them altogether, because there were two chickens and two rats) had arrived. I felt overwhelmed. What to feed them? How to house them? How to keep them warm at night? How much could they come out and play with our children? Could they walk on the beach? (Below you can see a photo of me holding Tamaiti and Hohepa on their first visit to our beach, and on page 31 the

photo a few moments later of the slightly confused reactions of Tamaiti, Hohepa, and Moana when I put them down on the sand.) Could they play on the lawn? Would they play with one another? Would they be happy? I thought of it like an adoption, and I put myself in the place of the person (each of these animals was a personality) being adopted: "Where am I? Who are these people to me? Why does it feel so strange? I miss my old home." Thoughts of this nature could well be occurring to the animals, too, at some level, though of course not necessarily in words. Isn't it an odd prejudice that so many people believe you cannot feel something unless it is articulated in speech?

The turmoil of this first week was extreme. I had been warned that there would be a certain amount of chaos and confusion. But thinking about chaos and confusion and experiencing them are quite different things. Unfamiliar noises, unfamiliar smells, unfamiliar foods. Kids coming in and out of the house, carrying one animal or another; other kids coming back in with a different animal; me trying ineffectually to impose order and rules: "Don't put the rat into your mouth, Ilan!" (Only much later did I learn that this is the favorite spot for the rat; she drinks from Ilan's tongue, much to his delight and my *continued* disbelief, not to mention disgust—what on earth is she drinking, and why does he like it so?) "Don't pick up the rabbit by his ears!" "Don't grab the chickens!" What had I been thinking to unleash this drama on our unsuspecting little community by the sea? Neighbors peered in our tall glass windows with horror at the chaos taking place inside in the large beach house filled with strange creatures.

When I look back at these early days of the project, I am most struck by how timid we all were. Even though I had considerable experience with animals, there was something about bringing them all together that made it much harder than I had anticipated to know what exactly we should do. Right away, we were not sure where Mika should sleep. We agonized over this for a long time. Should Mika be upstairs with us in our bedroom, or should she sleep with the other animals? What were the pros and cons of each location? What would Mika prefer? What would be best for the project? Should one trump the other? Should we use the aviary as a playpen or just for sleeping? Come to think of it, where should the other animals spend most of their day? In their enclosure? All together or separate? Could we allow them unsupervised playtime? At the beginning, we decided this was not a good idea. We simply did not know what might happen. Perhaps the dog would consume the chickens. Or the bunny might suffer a heart attack while being chased by the cat. Or the rat would die of fright when the chickens pecked at it. Anything could happen. Should we separate some of the animals? Could we allow the rats and the bunny to be together, but not the dog and the cat? Or should we be present at all encounters? Were we hoping for the animals to bond only with one another or with us as well? We didn't know what to expect. Initially, we decided to be cautious and were present as much as possible until we were certain the animals would not hurt one another. (Here we can see a photo of Robyn Haworth cautiously introducing Mika to Hohepa and Moa.)

————————

THE ADJUSTMENT PERIOD seemed to be easiest on the rats. Their very large wooden cage (originally designed for birds) had many different sleeping compartments, ladders, tunnels, and various inducements to play. My initial idea was for all the animals to be "exposed" to one another all day and night. But I could not risk letting the rats loose even in the huge enclosure we had built for the other animals, because there was little that could keep a rat from escaping. Perhaps they would have "chosen" not to escape, but if they did, they would have come to grief. I could not take the chance. But we had situated their cage inside the enclosure, so that the rats were visible to the other animals and the other animals were visible to the rats.

Contrary to expectations, Kia and Ora were very popular, at least with the children. Every child in the neighborhood came to visit with the rats. The rats enjoyed being handled, it seemed, and would come racing out of their little nest to be taken out when someone approached. Who would have thought children could love rats so much? But they do. They played with them by the hour. The parents would come by and make mock shudders: "A rat, how disgusting."

"What is disgusting?" I would ask them.

"The very idea."

"What is the idea?" I asked, genuinely curious at this odd turn of phrase. How, I wonder, can you be disgusted by the *idea* of a rat but quite like the furry little ratlet in front of you?

"Don't ask me to touch that 'thing,' " one mother said to me as her young daughter was kissing the rat all over his little body. "Just look at that tail! It's a naked tail! It's utterly monstrous." It was actually the same as the cute tail on the kitten, only this one lacked fur. Why should that make such a difference? It did, though. People seemed to have to *overcome* revulsion to bare tails.

A tiny poodle from the neighborhood almost made short work of one of the rats. Ilan showed Kia to the dog, thinking he would sniff her in friendly interest. Instead he ran at Ilan, who dropped the rat, and the dog rushed at her as if to eat her. To my surprise, the rat leapt at the nose of the dog and the dog took off in panic! Ilan did not know that dogs would attack rats. "I thought only cats are the enemies of rats," he said. Animals, I tried to explain to him, don't have the concept of enemy; with them only prey—that is, food—is the issue. Perhaps I am wrong; there may sometimes be enmities, but surely not categorical ones. It cannot be that every dog thinks, All cats are my enemy, because some cats and dogs are good friends. So how do we expand the concept of "family" that is the purpose of this book?

I was not keen on the concept of "natural enmity," but I saw that we had our hands full when it came to the older cats. Megala and Moko were now three years old, fully mature cats. They were sleek, healthy, active hunters. How would I *ever* be able to explain to them the concept of the peaceable kingdom? I tried. Had they been able to laugh out loud, they would have.

As it was, they left the room with supreme indifference. You know, somewhere I read that a command must be repeated at least two thousand times before a dog "gets" it. Is that number just elevated for cats, or do they simply not care?

In any case, I was faced with the challenge of how to protect the young animals from the older cats. I found a golden cage, a large, floorless playpenlike structure that I could stand in and that reached up to my waist, from which the chickens and rabbits couldn't get out. (Ilan and Manu loved to sit in it with the animals. One day I saw them drag it down to the beach and then go back and get each animal one by one out of the enclosure and take them into the cage; then they both got in and told the assorted creatures to behave themselves and become, *tout de suite,* a peaceable kingdom!) We put it on the beach that first week and introduced Moa and Moana to the ocean. Never having been on a beach before, they seemed a little confused. But not for long. Soon they were pecking the sand and seashells and pebbles, which was good, because they needed grist, and the calcium from the seashells was good for them. When we first put the rats on the sand, however, they ran for our legs and wanted to crawl up our trousers. Of course. How dumb of me: They were afraid of being easy prey in the open with no cover. An ancient instinct. They trusted us to protect them, and what is more, they already seemed to like us immensely. Why that should have been was a bit of a mystery to me. Was it because, like us, they are a sociable species? But chickens are an equally sociable species, and Moa and Moana were not nearly as friendly to us, at least not so far. Of course, it was still only the first week.

Speaking of chickens, Ilan wanted to know when he would see his first egg. Good question. "But Dad, I thought you were an animal expert. Don't you know something as simple as that?" he asked. Another good question. A call to George provided the answer: They first lay at five to six months. So we could expect to see eggs in three months' time. The idea filled Ilan with excitement. I felt it, too; there *is* something exciting about a chicken laying an egg. Such a little miracle. If both chickens were male, they obviously wouldn't lay eggs, but even if both chickens were female, they would. But the eggs would hatch only if one of our chickens was a rooster. Ilan was hoping that Moa was a rooster, for he wanted a chick to hatch and imprint on him. What exactly we would do with baby chicks was not something we had yet answered or even anticipated.

The chickens seemed to be singing. Just like birds. Well, they *are* birds after all, so it was not surprising. Yet I did not expect to hear a song; I thought their only sounds would have been a simple "cluck cluck cluck." This shows how little we listen.

I asked George, "Do all chickens sing?"

"Oh yes," he answered. "Some more than others, but they all like to make little reassuring sounds to one another. I guess you could call it singing."

To add to the confusion of that first week, we had a sudden rain. Rain! I hadn't thought about that for the chickens (Mika and Tamaiti came into the house; Hohepa the rabbit had his burrow to retreat to; he had dug himself a hole in the dirt in the enclosure, and he went in there whenever he felt like it). But I was the father, the adult; they were the children. It was my job to foresee problems. Why had I not thought of keeping the chickens out of the rain? I ran to the hardware store and bought a roomy wooden box, which I put in the enclosure that the chickens shared with the other animals. But they wouldn't enter the box. What spooked the "chooks" (as New Zealanders call chickens, and which yields a satisfying "chook-chook-chook" for calling them) in there? I called a carpenter, who, bless his heart, came the next day and built a nice roof over the enclosure. (See photo below of Hohepa on top of the roof in the enclosure.) They ran in out of the rain immediately and gave a satisfied chuckle.

I could not but be struck by the completely different personalities of these two chickens. How could they be so unalike? They came from the same mother, and they looked identical. Yet Moa was outgoing, friendly, with an open attitude, while Moana was suspicious, timid, and hesitant. I knew of no experiences in their early life that could have accounted for such a conspicuous difference. I hated to admit it, because I had such belief in the influence of learning and environment and how a benign early childhood primes us for goodness later in life. I did not like to think that we are born with an unalterable character that can only be modified, never changed, in later life. So I projected this same belief onto the chickens and the other animals. But I was not certain. Perhaps this experiment would clarify the matter for me.

———————

SOMEBODY ASKED if we were running a play center. What a great compliment. Play centers are a New Zealand innovation: Parents train for several weeks to learn about the needs of small children and how best to play with them, and then they come together two or three mornings a week with other parents. There is no cost, and the children love it. Manu goes to one. Well, often it felt as though our house had indeed become a play center, a special one for children and animals. Word of the animals had spread around the neighborhood, and on a typical day we could have as many as fourteen children visiting. There are mysteries hidden in the relation between children and animals. Children seem to grasp something essential about animals and our emotional connection to them that adults are apt to forget. "Cute," the kids would say, and we dismiss this term as if it were of no consequence. But in fact it is consequential. They perceive the similarity of these young animals to their own young selves: Scientists call it "neoteny," a kind of persisting juvenile charm. It evolves, obviously, so that adults will like, protect, and cherish children in spite of all the bother. Neotenous animals look cute for a reason. They *are* cute for a reason. Adults sometimes forget this, but kids don't. They are more in tune with neoteny in other species than we are. In fact, they understood the concept before scientists even had a word for it. The term *neoteny* is of fairly recent origin (my word processor's spell checker, for example, does not recognize it).

The animals seemed to (why do I hedge here? there is no "seem"—they *did*!) love the attention. Everyone vied to play with the rats, and Ilan and Manu built mazes and tunnels on the beach for them. Some of the neighborhood kids devised a neat little jungle on the beach for the chooks. They put them in the golden cage, and then they planted little bamboo sticks and driftwood inside. Moa and Moana obliged by stepping through as if it were their own primeval forest.

———————

WE KNEW that we wanted, as soon as possible, to introduce the animals to the beauty of our little beach paradise. (See page 41 for a photo of Gary Reese and me with Mika and Hohepa.)

Our beach walk was a tradition every day, and it was certainly one of our goals to be able to walk down to the huge pohutukawa tree at the end of the beach with the animals and watch them play in the branches or on the sand. At low tide, we had lots of little tidal pools and bare rocks the animals could inspect, and the cats and dog could run into the lush bank covered in native bushes and trees. If we walked even farther, we came to a little rock hill we could climb and proceed to the next beach over from ours, one that had no houses on it and was usually deserted. It was, in all, about a half-mile walk, but one I was sure the cats and dog, at least, would come to treasure. I was right. But soon the rats began to like it when I put them in my sleeve and went for long strolls on the beach. Even grownups began to come by on almost a daily basis and ask to take the rats for a walk. I think people (at least some people) enjoyed having their prejudices proven wrong.

We constantly enriched the rats' cages with new objects to keep them interested. I began to notice things about rats that I had never seen before, such as what perfect little ears they have and how much pleasure I took in looking at them. Their ears are diaphanous and very delicate. I liked to rub them gently between my fingers, and the rats liked it when I did that, making a purring sound to indicate they were happy. (Is it possible, though, that they were actually protesting?)

I took such joy in hearing the sounds of pleasure from the rats and the chickens. I hadn't yet heard such a sound from Hohepa the rabbit, though. Come to think of it, I had heard no sound at all from Hohepa. Did rabbits ever vocalize? I heard once that they emit a terrible scream when they are slaughtered. Thank God I will never hear it. But I wondered if Hohepa would have any sound to indicate happiness.

The older cats seemed to be adjusting to everybody, with the exception of the rats. That may have been asking too much of them. In fact, I had been dreading introducing Tamaiti to the rats. The sooner it was done, however, the better the chance they would get along. (I was afraid of an "accident.") Finally, I tried it. I put Kia into the palm of my hand and slowly approached the sleeping Tamaiti.

Kia leapt out of my hand and straight up into the air, landed, and then raced away at tremendous speed. When we caught her, her little heart was thumping wildly. Then,

strangely, she seemed to forget her fear, and she and Tamaiti
nuzzled noses. So fast? Odd. As if the first reaction were her
instinct coming into play (not *as if*, it *was*) and the second her
more considered view: "Hmm, not such a bad little cat after
all." How else to explain this unusual behavior? I was curious
to see if it would last or which would prevail, nature or nurture.

It was, after all, in the nature of the rat to fear the cat. Or
was it? Was this something rats learned, painfully, from experience, or were they born knowing to avoid cats? Little Kia may
have been hardwired to feel fear, but she seemed to learn almost
immediately that there *was* nothing to fear in spite of what her
"nature" or her instincts told her. Could this benign experience
alter the wiring in her brain? We would see.

Mika the dog and Tamaiti the cat acted as if they already
owned the house. Hohepa was still resisting the temptations of
indoor living, but after several weeks, Moa and Moana dared to
come inside. I loved the thought of the chickens having the run
of the house. Would they ever venture up the stairs and visit me
in my office where I worked on my computer?

Shortly after I wrote that last sentence, as if on cue, they
hopped up the stairs, walked into my office, perched in my
bookshelf (see the photo on page 44 with Manu pointing at
them), and watched while I sat and worked at the computer on
this very passage! True, I had not thought about the huge
amount of chicken droppings they would leave behind. Chickens poop wherever they feel like it, and that included right on
top of my books or bookshelves or even on my desk. I didn't

know how to make my wishes clear to them or whether there was any chance of success. I decided to simply cope: I kept a large box of tissues in the living room (see page 45 for a photo of the chickens wandering about our living room) and up in my office and used them constantly to clean up after them. (Is there a fortune to be made in chicken diapers? I would be the first customer.)

In fact, the chickens were turning out to be the hardest of the animals to "tame." Odd word, that. We use it to mean two very different things. There is a difference between tameness and domesticity; all of the animals in this experiment were domesticated. When we say they are becoming more "tame," we simply mean that they are getting more used to us. It is not that we have "tamed" a wild animal (which sometimes hap-

pens, but far more rarely). I would almost certainly not succeed in this project with animals that were truly wild—that is, not feral chickens (domestic chickens who have reverted to the wild), but wild red Burmese jungle fowl. They would have been far too timid, too "wild," if you will, to ever allow contact with a human. (We also use the word *wild* in two different senses: one to mean an animal who lives without contact with humans and another to recognize that some domesticated animals are less compliant than others.)

A wild chicken could probably *never* be tamed and would almost certainly never accept another animal as a friend, no matter what the circumstances. Why? Well, for one thing they would have no overwhelming desire to please us, as a dog does, for example. Dogs are probably the most domesticated of all animal species, meaning that their behavior toward us, and even toward other animals, has been influenced by what we want from them.) For another, their survival instinct would be too strong to override. Our chickens had seen a great deal of us, and we took them each day in their little playpen, the golden cage, down to the beach and to the grass, so that they had plenty of variety. They didn't panic, and after a few minutes they would sit still in our arms, but the next time we went to pick them up it would be as if they had never seen us before. Was it simply a question of time, or was something more basic and less plastic at work here?

I talked to the previous owner (I'd like to stop using that word!) of the chickens, to learn how best to pick them up. He told me to slide my hand under their bottoms and let them rest on my hand. "They should like that," he said. But, he added—sagaciously, I thought: "You need to learn as much as they do. They have to learn to like being handled, and you have to learn how to handle them." I thought that was great. Here is a man who has learned from chickens.

Tamaiti the kitten was ceaselessly pouncing on poor Hohepa the rabbit inside the enclosure, which made it difficult for the rabbit to escape. (See photo on page 47.) He seemed to think Hohepa was not a rabbit, but another kitten. It was a game for Tamaiti. But it wasn't clear if Hohepa was aware of this or that he even cared. He wore the long-suffering look of one who knows no escape. He seemed to have not yet emerged from the state of mild shock he was in the first day we took him away from his mother

and siblings (as I write this, I wonder what animal, human or other, would *not* be). As this was only his first week, I was eager to see how he would respond in the weeks to come. Of course, he would grow rapidly: In six months he would be nearly full grown, and since he was a Flemish giant, that meant he would eventually reach twenty-five pounds! I didn't think any cat would want to tangle with him at that point.

The biggest problem, just as I suspected, was my two older cats, Moko and Megala. They spent all day staring at the rats and the chickens. (See page 48 for a photo of Moko meeting Kia for the first time.) They were not happy about Tamaiti, either, or the puppy. Only Hohepa seemed not to interest them. I had never meant them to be part of the experiment, to get them used to the other animals, since I was sure I couldn't teach an old cat

new tricks, but it was my hope that they would surprise me and eventually accept the younger animals. Or at least remain indifferent. It would be delightful, though, if they could learn to enjoy them. Could that happen? Most cats, I knew from my reading and from my own experience, were reluctant to accept *any* other animal into their lives, even another cat. Strange, isn't it, that they so readily accept a new human. For Mika, it seemed just the opposite. He would positively grovel at the sight of *any* strange dog but was leery of new people. Again I suspected this might have had something to do with his first weeks as a stray puppy on the streets of a rather tough neighborhood.

FEEDING THE ANIMALS was proving to be more of a challenge than I thought. How do you discover what rats and rabbits love to eat, except by trying everything? Surely it was not cheating to make the animals like me by offering them their favorite food. That was a simple matter with a dog or a cat, but not with a chicken. I soon discovered, for example, that the chickens were not nearly as fond of the feed you can buy for them in a pet store as they were of various greens and grains we already had around our house. I would never have known that rabbits go crazy for young bamboo shoots (just like panda bears) if somebody had not brought some along; we watched in amazement as Hohepa went through it like a lawn mower. Nor could I have imagined that the rats' favorite drink was soy milk, until I offered it, on a whim, only to have them slurp it up like kids finishing an ice-cream soda. Hohepa felt the same about dandelions. The chooks were always on the lookout for any poor stray cockroach. Wham! They were on him, and he was history. And so we learned that chickens are not vegetarians.

In the early weeks, all the animals preferred to be fed than played with. Nevertheless, I tried to play with them as well. I would lie down in their enclosure and hope they would come to investigate the strange being prone in their space. But they simply avoided me. They also avoided one another. That was not the idea; they were supposed to "interact." But you cannot force intimacy. Maybe it can only be earned. I was prepared to do whatever it would take so that these animals would want to be in my company and in one another's, but what would it take? "Patience," Leila urged.

The word continued to spread around the neighborhood and beyond—kids were showing up all the time, some from blocks away, wanting to see the animals in what they began to call "the experiment." I wish now I had thought from the beginning of a better word for what I was doing. I had no problems with the children coming, as I reasoned the more the animals saw of people the better. The children often brought their dogs, and that too was a good thing. Socialization: I could not get enough of it. Constant benign exposure to the world—what could be better for anybody, human or animal? The animals seemed to share my opinion.

I think the kids who visited loved this experiment because they intuitively knew the value of this kind of exposure, from their own lives or from school. Many people, even adults, still come on a constant basis. I found that as interesting as the animals. Why do people love to watch animals so much, especially animals making friends across the species barrier? It is more than simple curiosity. What hunger in us does this attest to?

TWO

REALITY SETS IN
(TROUBLE IN PARADISE)

IN PRACTICALLY EVERY ZOO in the country, the philosophical mood is in favor of creating the most natural conditions possible for all the animals. The idea is to learn what sort of environment the animals are used to or have been evolved to live in and re-create it to whatever extent one can. It is a worthy goal, but one that is never achievable in its entirety. How do you replicate the vast spaces that elephants are used to wandering in, to take just one obvious example? The goal is admirable, but it seems beyond the reach of a zoo.

I knew that all zoos and aquariums have adopted the principle that no cage should remain without enrichment in the form of toys or mazes or objects and a varied routine to lessen the boredom of living in captivity. In a zoo, this is a step forward. It makes good psychological sense. But the very fact that it was needed, I used to argue, is weighty evidence against any form of captivity. Now, though, I was thinking about enrichment for the chickens in their enclosure, so I was forced to recognize that I too was indulging in a form of captivity, even if one very different from that of a zoo. I needed to create an optimal environment for them short of absolute freedom.

So I called Robyn Haworth, a neighbor, friend, and devoted animal person, and she came over with her two teenage children and immediately set about improving the space (it was really quite large, about two hundred square feet): They brought an old mailbox for the chickens and put straw into it to form a nest. Then they decided the plants growing in the enclosure were not healthy, so they dug them up. I brought buckets of sand to lay down in part of the enclosure to make available to them the minerals of the sea in the seashells. The kids constructed a ramp for the chickens to go up and down on. They were able now to stand on the edge of their enclosure, surveying the yard. I was tempted to give them more freedom. I knew I could leave them in front of the house or on the beach, and they would stay around and come back home in the evening. That is what happens on the old-fashioned family farm. But too many dogs came down to the beach, and I could not always be watching. I loved to think of them knowing their home already, though. It was almost a matter of pride for me: "Aw, they know where they belong."

Can individuals do any better with their companion animals than zoos? We do strive for it. We are not comfortable with narrow confinement for any animal. I wanted to compensate my animals in particular for subjecting them to this somewhat unnatural (if benign) experiment. Rabbits and cats would not seek each other out in the wild, and if I wanted them to do so in my house, I should at least offer them better lives than they would normally have in a human household. If the chickens cooperated with me and allowed proximity with other animals and with humans, they too should be rewarded in some fashion. For me the philosophical issue was simple: For animals to be as happy as they could be, they needed to live in circumstances as close to natural as possible. Those were the conditions I wanted to create.

―――――

WITH ONE BIG EXCEPTION, of course: peaceableness. Nature does not generally provide peaceful coexistence. So now I had run up against what must confront every researcher: the disparity between what you set out to do and what you can realistically achieve. My experiment, to find the peaceable kingdom, was really in conflict with allowing the animals to live as close to a natural life as could be achieved in the suburbs of a large city. What was good for me was not necessarily good for the animals. If I chose the former over the latter, how different would I be from any other researcher who rationalizes inflicting pain and suffering on animals for the greater good—namely, knowledge or human benefit? Even if the rationalization was patently untrue, the researcher could believe it and use it to justify the cruelty.

The chickens were giving me problems. One day just about a month after the beginning of the project, I woke up with a feeling of despair: How could this possibly work? I thought. How would the chickens ever interact with the other animals when they still avoided *me* as if I were out to eat them? (Silly them, right? Who would ever think such a thing?) To my surprise and delight, though, there came a day not too long after when for the first time the chickens did not run away from me when I approached. Moreover, they started to enjoy their environment, climbing into the small palm tree in the yard and pecking at the window to get my attention when I was in the house.

Giving the chickens a good and natural life meant taking them out of their enclosure more and more until they could be out most of the day. After all, they were hunter-gatherers, like us. They wanted to be out and about. They kept fairly close to the house, wandering out on the beach and into the neighbor's yard and not much farther, but I was concerned about being able to control their movement. Suppose they decided to take up residence in somebody else's yard miles from here? Could I give them their freedom and keep my experiment running?

Freedom for the chickens was one issue; for the rats, it was an entirely different matter. For their own safety, freedom was not something I could give the rats. They would have been eaten in days, if not hours or minutes, by the cats. But I could keep them on my desk, where they would explore each book and taste each pencil, and the family could have them with us while we watched videos in the evening, when they are most active. I still had to protect them from Megala, the older cat, whose primary goal in life now, it seemed, was to catch them. That protection was somewhat artificial, for there are no rat guardians in the real world. On the other hand, in their own real world, rats have one another and deep underground burrows to slip into in times of danger. They are never exposed as nakedly as they were in our house. Moreover, rats are far more guarded in the wild, constantly on the alert for possible danger. With us, Kia and Ora relaxed that instinct. I wasn't sure if their ability to do that came from breeding, experience, or a combination of both. Ilan began carrying the rats around in his sleeve; Leila had them in her blouse; and I had them in the hood of my sweatshirt. Each time I passed the cats or the dog, I would allow them to sniff the rats, and the rats would sniff back. They were very cautious initially, but soon they seemed to recognize the other animals and were clearly less frightened. Conditioning was beginning its work.

Hohepa was friendly with everyone or, rather, seemed to have no negative feelings toward any of the other animals, but I had not yet found a way to allow him to roam about, either, because he would run away. He did not seem to have the same sense of "home" that the chickens possessed. He would go anywhere, seemingly. I was not sure what went on in his mind, or even in his peregrinations, since I could not follow him. He would quickly disappear into the shrubbery, and then I would have to wait until he made a sudden reappearance. Perhaps he had an internal map whose contours I was ignorant of. Perhaps in time we would come to know what he thought of his surroundings. For the moment, in those early days, he was still a mystery, and we were unsure how to handle him. This was in contrast with the man who gave him to me, who insisted that rabbits needed absolutely nothing but their food to be happy. "Keep him in a small cage all the time; he won't mind." In his view, Hohepa *had* no mind. But I was convinced that we had merely not yet succeeded in entering the mind of this animal. I was not sure we ever would, but I would continue to try as long as he lived with us.

Because of their species' long association with humans, the dog and the kitten posed fewer problems, or rather problems of a different nature. Tamaiti could do whatever he liked, because what he liked seemed to correspond almost exactly with what *we* wanted. He moved from room to room and person to person, seeking fun and play. He appeared to be without an ounce of malice. He liked everything and everybody equally. (On page 57 and 58 you can see him getting acquainted for the first time with Kia and Ora.) He was delighted to meet up with one of us and just as delighted to meet up with Mika or one of the older cats. These cats, on the other hand, had altogether different ideas and ran away from him with a hiss and a snarl. But the hisses began to get less acrimonious over time. Perhaps Megala and Moko, too, were succumbing to his charm. Tamaiti seemed genuinely puzzled when they ran off, as if to say, "What is it about me you don't like?" Incapable of any aggression himself,

he evidently did not comprehend it in others. A nice trait, I must say. Would the older cats find it contagious?

I suppose I was a little nervous as I waited for Tamaiti to grow up—concerned that he would move from innocence to malign adult. Of course, it is unfair to say that aggression in cats is bad. Cats have no evil intentions toward prey; their only intention is to eat. But I did not want Tamaiti to see the bunny as food. So even though there were days when he played with Hohepa most of the afternoon, I remained wary of Tamaiti's intentions. It looked like play, but I worried that it might instead be hunting preparations, that it could turn nasty eventually or at some moment when I would not be there to stop it. Could some atavistic instinct kick in, making a mockery of my experiment, showing me how defenseless I truly was, faced with a force of nature?

I was not sure what I would then do. Would I admit defeat immediately or attempt to wrestle with instinct? How much faith, after all, was I prepared to place in the reassurances of a "breeder" that rag dolls simply do not hunt? Cats are cats, regardless of the breed.

Our two older cats, Moko and Megala, were even more unpredictable. You could not simply walk up to them and pick them up or stroke them. They would struggle to free themselves, and if you persisted, they would lash out at you. And of course it was a formula for humiliation should you decide that you wanted them to come when you called them and to stay when you told them to. They would look briefly astonished, as if wondering if you had mistaken them for dogs, and then pointedly ignore you. But should *they* decide they wanted to be affectionate, they would come and rub against your leg and look up at you beseechingly or snuggle under the covers all night long. I warned visitors not to expect their beauty to be complemented by gentle and affectionate behavior. "They might well scratch you," I would say. At which point, of course, looking stricken at my unjust warning, the cats would approach the visitor and with a plaintive meow ask to be lifted up and stroked, at the same time giving me a sly look while the visitor decided I did not know my own cats. Fascinating.

I find it so difficult to understand just what goes on in their complex little minds. Moko and Megala *pretended* that Tamaiti was the bane of their existence. How could I have brought this kitten into *their* house? But slowly it became clear that they actually enjoyed playing with him. Of course, they could not admit such a thing openly, certainly not to me and perhaps not even to themselves. I have always claimed that animals do not have unconscious emotions, but here was a circumstance that suggested I might be wrong.

Dogs are much easier for us to understand. Perhaps they recognized long ago that humans are a bit challenged emotionally, so they decided to make it easy for us: Tail wagging means happy. Their faces look mournful when they are feeling sad. Few people have trouble understanding what a dog is feeling. Cats never bothered to make themselves transparent. To this day, many people believe cats feel nothing.

Perhaps it is this quintessential difference between dogs and cats that allows dogs to adjust to human ways more easily. Where cats often display resistance (in the classical therapeutic sense), dogs are masters at compliance and taking in the feelings of others. Perhaps this makes them more open to other species as well. Baxter, a two-year-old white miniature poodle living with our friend and neighbor Conny Lo (who was taking a course at the university in canine behavior), was an example of how emotional education is uncomplicated for an intelligent, sensitive dog. Conny was interested in our experiment from the beginning, but when she first brought Baxter by our house to visit with all the animals, he behaved as expected: He chased the cat, tried to eat the rat, leapt at the chickens and bunny, and gave no indication that he would be able to understand what we wanted of him. I thought it was hopeless, but Conny knew him better. For when it seemed to dawn on him what we were doing, he made the appropriate adjustments, as if a light bulb had gone on in his bright little head: "Oh, I get it; they want us to be friends. I can do that!" And he did. We really did not do anything to force him or even to persuade him. I think it was pure observation. He saw, and he became interested. So at first he tried to make friends with Hohepa, who initially would have nothing to do with him, and he also wanted to befriend the two older cats, who were even less welcoming. Tamaiti, on the other hand, was always up for a new friend, and they played, not wildly, but peacefully. While it is not surprising that dogs have this capacity, it is nonetheless interesting to see it happen before your eyes.

Baxter's ability to play with Tamaiti did not stem simply from a desire to please us, as I initially thought. That may have been a component, but it was clear he also *liked* playing with Tamaiti. In this way he was able to enlarge his own emotional world, and I don't doubt that he knew it. Dogs are capable of getting such pleasure that they are always seeking new objects upon which to practice this seemingly infinite capacity for enjoyment. Yet as far as I know, no wolf has ever made friends with an animal from another species, even though wolves and dogs are almost identical when it comes to behavior. Could this be because we supply dogs and not wolves with the opportunity (not part of their genetic heritage) that enlarges their own lives?

I KNEW I had to spend considerable time with each animal if I was to get to know him or her intimately. So one day I decided to spend all day with the chickens on the beach. (You can see us in the photo on page 62.) For a while, I just sat and read. Then I dozed in the sun. As the day wore on, they too settled down and seemed much more relaxed than I had ever seen them, as if to say, "Finally you know what to do with us." They dug a little hollow in the sand and lay in it with a look of complete ease. Their whole body language spoke of a lack of fear. They would get up from time to time and wander down to the shore, there to scratch in the wet sand for sand hoppers. I felt honored that they were comfortable enough to relax with me.

It was a lazy and very satisfying day. Were somebody to ask me, "What do chickens want?" I feel I could answer with some authority: "To lie about in the sun on the beach with a friend."

My friend Robyn Haworth came by at the end of the day with an old discarded table to put into their enclosure at the back of the house. She had decided on her own that this would enrich the environment. I saw at once that she was right. Chickens are hardly minimalists, so we added little perches. The chickens loved them and seemed to know right away what they were there for. A most happy end to a good day. (Much later, I was to learn that the chickens were comfortable on my arm; they perched there as if in a tree. See page 63 for a photo of Anneke with Moana on her shoulder and Kia in her arm, and Rebecca holding Tamaiti and Moa on her shoulder.)

DJ, a four-and-a-half-year-old guide dog, was down on the beach with the chickens one day and gave them a quick glance that said, "I could eat those chickens if I felt like it, but Mark and Jo, the people I live with and take care of, don't want me to, so I won't." That made me realize that we want to teach all our animals new rules and new boundaries—but expanding boundaries, not ones that confine them; we want them to be as comfortable as possible with their natural enemies. After all, everyone needs to learn certain house rules, even Ilan, and everyone, including the animals and Ilan, is somewhat resistant. Yet everybody wants rules.

A few days earlier, Raven, our neighbor who lives with Fuzzbucket, the tame nine-month-old magpie, had an idea for using a cat harness for Hohepa the rabbit. That way we could

walk him and he could get exercise, but we would not risk his running off and being attacked by a strange dog. At first when we put it on, he tried to shake it off. But while he didn't like it, he seemed to accept it (and most other things) with equanimity. And within a few days of being introduced to the harness, Hohepa spent two hours on a leash with Raven, who confessed to having fallen in love with him.

I was still searching for ways to give the animals a better—that is, freer—life. We had the idea of fencing in the whole front yard for the chickens and Hohepa, but this would not help with the rats, who could have just slipped through. The rats were still underprivileged compared with everyone else. In these early weeks, they never got to be free outdoors, even briefly. There seemed no way to avoid a cage of some kind for them. I wondered if I was to take that as a signal that they were not meant to be kept at all. I knew I had to figure out a better way.

On many days there were at least ten kids here, and each would take an animal to play with, even the chickens. They would carry the animals about and take them to the beach; they would make little sand castles for them and bring them right up to the edge of the water or take them on short walks along the shore. I urged them to bring the different animals together with one another as much as possible. I also wanted them to get used to different smells and the feel of different people. I wanted these animals to feel comfortable with one another *and* with us, to come to accept not only all the animals as "family," but also the various humans who could come by, especially those who would do so on a regular basis. It was not only children who visited; there were days when ten or twelve adults came by as well to see the animals. The animals seemed to enjoy it.

Being a lapcat, Tamaiti was not supposed to love the beach, but he did. He liked to run sideways, and when he reached you, he would leap straight into the air. It was an impressive trick and never failed to elicit oohs and aahs from whatever audience was present. That, evidently, was the point, for Tamaiti would then swagger away, satisfied at his reception. He would positively gloat in applause. He loved to entertain.

The chickens had taken to standing by the door of their courtyard, either to watch us or to alert us to them, as if they wanted to be near us. When I took them to the beach early in the morning and let them run around, within seconds they were scratching in the sand and digging. The most wonderful sign of trust: A seagull cried loudly near them and they jumped, ran to me, and stood behind me, as if they recognized that I would protect them. Such pusillanimous language: because they *knew* I would protect them. There, that's better.

I was still searching for a compromise, though, between what I was trying to do, *my* agenda, and what the animals themselves would have liked. In a previous book, *The Pig Who Sang to the Moon: The Emotional World of Farm Animals,* I stated that the most important thing we can ask about any animal is: What makes that animal happy? Animal scientists have often thrown up their hands in despair, as if we could never find the answer to such a complex question. Not true. It is actually a fairly simple question to answer. We *all* know the answer: An animal is happy when doing what the animal evolved to do in the natural world. Any restriction on space, on relations, on longevity, creates conditions for unhappiness. A chicken who is able to live for up to fifteen years in the wild never, under captive conditions, lives to anything like that. The average life for a "broiler chicken" (the hideous but honest term we use for chickens who are destined to be barbecued) is forty-five days. For a hen laying eggs it is never more than a few years. You cannot argue that you are giving animals a happy life when you kill them long before they are even mature. How much moral intelligence does it take to realize this is wrong?

Because in this project I had gathered together animals who would not normally choose to be together, I had to put certain restrictions on their movements. How could I see to it that I acknowledged their preferences and yet not lose the entire rationale of the project, which was to see if they would, against the odds, not merely tolerate one another, but become friends? I was not sure it was possible. Here I could see the dilemma that animal researchers sooner or later face. What they want to know is rarely compatible with the optimum well-being of the animal. Compromise is inevitable, and once we are sliding around on that slippery slope, it does not take much before we find ourselves getting further and further away from our most cherished principles. Mine was: First the animals' happiness, then my curiosity.

Here is an example of what I mean: Hohepa the rabbit, while "friendly" (that is, completely without aggression or malice) and liked by everyone, appeared to be less sociable than the other animals. In the first weeks, even months, he gave no sign that he wanted to be with us or with any of the other animals. What he really seemed to want was to wander. He did not want to be confined. Could he have made himself any clearer? I wondered. He would take any opportunity to get out, and he wouldn't return. I had lived with a rabbit before, but never with one who was able to wander freely. Confined and treated as a house companion, my rabbit became friendly and sociable. Hopel Popel, as we called him, had the run of our house. He was a large white rabbit afraid of no other animal, especially our three dogs, whom he immediately intimidated into submission (it was a posture they retained for his entire sojourn in our house). He liked being with everybody: humans, cats, dogs. When the doorbell rang, he was the first to reach the door, happy to greet whoever came in, especially if he or she was accompanied by an animal companion. Weird? I don't know. I cannot be sure that Hopel Popel was not just a very unusual rabbit.

Perhaps there is a default behavioral gene for friendliness in house rabbits. I was sure, though, that Hohepa would not want to wander freely if it meant that the cat would jump him and chase him around his compound. I would have had no objection to his running about outside all day, on the beach, to the neighboring houses, into the forest, as long as he came back throughout the day and then spent the night here. But I didn't think this was likely. Hohepa was not going to reason with me or find a happy medium between what he wanted and what I wanted. Of all domestic animals, only dogs do that. And even they have to learn it slowly, over time; compromise does not come naturally even to them.

But even if Hohepa was not becoming friendly with me, he at least appeared to accept Mika. (In the photo on page 69 they are on my lap.) They came face-to-face, eating the same stalk of celery. Mika put her head between her paws and munched on the celery, while Hohepa did the same. Video camera, where were you when I needed you?

We had a terrible scare with Hohepa a month or so into the project. An English journalist was interviewing me for the BBC World Service, and she wanted a shot of the chickens walking on the beach. They were hiding inside our large dog kennel (which we had gotten for Mika but which she would never deign to enter), so to get them to emerge, she turned it on its side. It is very heavy. The chickens came out, and she followed them out onto the beach. I went to turn the dog kennel back upright when I saw a ghastly sight: Hohepa was trapped under the edge of the kennel, which must weigh at least fifty pounds. He lay immobile, panting. He was not in any obvious pain, and he could have just been traumatized, but I knew that rabbits do very poorly with great stress. I watched him closely over the next few hours, as I just couldn't see how such a heavy weight on his small back would

not break it. Rabbits have very tender spines and can easily be killed accidentally. Oh God, I could not bear the thought of Hohepa dying, but it did not look good. He was lying about, in one spot, still breathing very quickly. Could he possibly survive? Manu and Ilan were both crying; they were inconsolable.

It was late, and I could not reach a vet, so I called the rabbit man, who told me that from my description it was clear that Hohepa's back was broken and I should bring him by.

"Can you fix it?" I asked.

"No, I will kill him."

"No!"

"Believe me, it's the kindest thing you can do for him. He is in terrible pain, but there is no way you can know that, because rabbits just won't show it. Bring him right over and let me end his agony."

He made sense (how odd, though, to think that an animal is suffering and there are *no* signs at all). The thing is, I didn't trust this man. Everything he had ever said about rabbits indicated that he did not really care about them. Moreover, how could he be so certain of Hohepa's condition just from my phone call? There was no way I would allow Hohepa to be killed unless I was convinced there was no alternative. I told the man this.

"Well, monitor him until eight p.m., and if he is still sitting without moving, you have no choice."

People rarely have no choice, and the phrase bothered me. But I was nervous as evening arrived. Finally, it was eight, time for the call. But no, wait! Hohepa was moving, hopping! There was no way he could have done that with a broken back. He ran up to me and sniffed my hand, almost as if he were asking for a cuddle. He seemed as relieved as I was. I fed him his favorite foods, dandelion and nasturtiums, and he ate eagerly. He was better! He was cured! I felt so relieved. What I now think happened was that the kennel must have crushed him, but nothing was broken, he was only bruised, and he was now feeling better. When I called the journalist to tell her the news, she cried with relief. Everybody liked Hohepa. There was something appealing in his calmness, even though he appeared to be the least sociable of the animals.

What I learned from this experience is how little we know

about these animals. I speak for myself, first of all. After all, initially I did not even know that rabbits love nasturtiums. Now I know. But I still don't understand rabbit pain, and I wonder whether anyone does. Earlier I stated that there are no experts when it comes to human emotions or animal emotions. But this assumed there are experts when it comes to matters such as physical pain. Maybe that needs to be questioned as well. It is my principle never to believe a medical doctor (Leila excepted, of course) without getting a second and sometimes even a third opinion. I think I would apply the same rule to animal experts.

Soon after the incident with the kennel, there was a rainstorm, and I was worried that Hohepa would be miserable outside so cold and wet, so I brought him into the house. He seemed to like it. But when we were inside, Tamaiti, as usual, pounced on him and I think annoyed him. I was still not sure what annoys a rabbit. Rabbits rarely vocalize; making noise would be too dangerous for them in their natural state—they would only be calling attention to themselves, which is rarely a good thing for a prey species. But here in the house Hohepa tried to shake Tamaiti off, while Tamaiti rode on his back. It was play, but it was predator play, and while it might have been fun for the predator, I think it was less fun for the prey. Yet Hohepa is a domestic rabbit, not a wild rabbit; and while he may have *some* of the same instincts and behavior of the wild rabbit, he is more docile and less frightened—perhaps even less frightened of an animal who would ordinarily be a predator. I wondered if he would ever actually *like* Tamaiti and seek him out. It seemed unlikely, but I knew that only time would tell.

The whole project was turning out to be more of a challenge than I had thought. The household sometimes felt like a chaotic nursery rhyme come to life: the chicks pecking the rats, the kitten chasing the chicks, the dog chasing the cat, and everybody chasing the bunny. Would I really be able to create a peaceable kingdom in the end? Should I even be attempting to create a peaceable kingdom? The truth is, I did not mean this as merely a symbolic experiment. I was convinced that they, the animals themselves, would be happier, would benefit in the long run.

I was worried that the chickens were not perching sufficiently, so several children and I dragged a huge piece of driftwood into their courtyard so they could jump up into its many branches. I went to pick them up when they were perched on a branch above me, and they had no objection. What they *did* object to was being taken from above. It's clear why: That is what a predator does. When I got down to their level and they could look into my eyes, they were calmer.

We needed to be gentle with Moa and Moana, and they had to learn that we intended them no harm. The ways we have devised to pick up chickens are awful. I was sickened by footage I'd seen of men going through chicken warehouses, grabbing three or four of them by their feet, turning them upside down, and then walking away with them, often breaking their legs in the process. Picking up a chicken the right way requires patience; it must be slow. We want to come at them from below, giving them foot purchase, as if we were the branches of a tree and they could feel safe in our hands. Ilan was managing it well, and the chickens didn't seem to object whenever he came over to pick them up. They also enjoyed perching on sixteen-year-old Anneke's head (she and Rebecca came down several times a week to help with the care of the animals). Maybe they had a sense of humor. Their eyes, which I seldom saw because they were covered by their feathers, were so black that I could not read them. I needed to find other ways to learn what they liked to eat, how to hold them, and what would make them happy.

It is interesting how long it takes to find out what makes a chicken happy, or a rat, or even a rabbit. We do not know them the way we know dogs and cats. How could I have known that chickens loved broccoli? And what about the chickens' favorite food? Well, it turned out to be crushed macadamia nuts. A man walking along the beach saw me playing with the chickens and called out: "Have you ever fed them crushed macadamia nuts? Try it; you will be surprised at their reaction." He was right: They positively gorged on them. Then they discovered sand hoppers (those small, transparent flylike insects found under dry seaweed), which they scratched out from their hiding places on the beach. I had thought chickens were vegetarians. I was wrong, for apparently live food tastes better to them than anything else. I thought rabbits were *pure* vegetarians, but yesterday I saw Hohepa munching away at the cat food. Oh well, it is my philosophy not to impose my own wishes on the animals (or even on my children). They have to come to their preferences and beliefs (if animals have beliefs about food) on their own.

After dragging the driftwood into the enclosure for Moa and Moana to perch on, I realized how important perching was to them and how much they must enjoy it. The chickens perched on my arms, my head, wherever they found purchase, and soon I had everyone interested in improving the animals' surroundings, enriching their environment. They saw what a big difference the driftwood made to the chickens.

I still did not know how much freedom I could allow Moa and Moana. Freedom on the beach was the ultimate "enrichment." I had spent a lot of time catching them after a few minutes of freedom, until I realized this was unnecessary. A few weeks earlier, I had let them loose on the beach with me for two hours, and they stuck close to me. They ignored Mika and Tamaiti, who were also on the beach, but clearly they were not ignoring me; they kept me very much in sight. Sometimes the subtlety of the interaction with the other animals escaped me. It was there, I was convinced, but I seemed to fail to notice. How I wished they could explain their feelings to me.

———

THE DAY AFTER we dragged the driftwood into their enclosure, we found out that the chickens could fly. As I was walking out of the enclosure, I heard a rush of wings and turned to see both chickens in the air, flying up to the top branch. Only a few weeks into our "experiment," each day seemed to bring new revelations. They may not have been able to fly far, or high, but flying it was. I wondered whether it gave them pleasure and whether they were as surprised as I was: "Look, I can fly!" They are birds, after all, so why was I so surprised?

As it turned out, they didn't spend all their time hunting and gathering, not by a long shot. I realized this by spending most of another day with them toward the end of the first month. A good part of the time they lay stretched out on the beach. I watched them dust-bathe, actually dirt-bathe, and it was really amazing. It gave them so much joy; it infected me with the same feeling. They used their wings like little shovels to scoop the dirt up into their feathers. They fluffed their feathers and made sure the dirt got all the way down to their skin. Then they flattened their feathers, trapping the dirt inside. They stayed still then, letting the dirt do its work, for at least ten minutes. Then they stood up and shook all the dirt out of their feathers. This elaborate procedure removes the stale oil from their feathers, and they then use their beaks to take fresh oil from a gland at the base of their tails and distribute it through their feathers, waterproofing them. It was fascinating to watch the intricacy of something that most people never notice and that seemed to give them much satisfaction. Moa and Moana would do everything a wild bird does, given the opportunity. Not only do we generally deny chickens that opportunity, we compound our sin by refusing to inform ourselves of what they are actually capable of.

For the longest time, I had no luck convincing the chickens they should be friends with rats. Is it that chickens know rats eat eggs? The chickens pecked at the rats and even chased them. How, I wondered, can we have a peaceable kingdom if I can't convince the chickens to behave otherwise? How do you change a chicken's mind? I hoped that their experience with the gentle giant (me) would prevail and turn them into friends. We would just have to wait and see. Meanwhile, I had to make sure the chickens didn't harm them. The rats were so small that they seemed especially vulnerable. Hohepa the bunny was fine with them; mostly he ignored them, but sometimes he would give them a short but friendly little sniff or let one of them go for a ride on his back. Tamaiti, though, seemed not entirely sure he didn't want to eat those rats. The big cats, of course, were certain: They did want to eat the rats (the pleasure it gives me to use the past tense here will be explained later). I could not imagine that they would ever change their minds. On the other hand, what has supposition to do with inquiry? I vowed to keep an open mind.

Sometimes my suppositions were confirmed. For example, I had always enjoyed taking walks on the beach with my older cats, Moko and Megala. I had all along been hoping they would continue this habit once they got used to Mika the puppy tagging along on our stroll. For the first month after the "others" (as they no doubt refer to them) came into our lives, Moko and Megala boycotted this ritual, causing me much sorrow. Then one day, as I set off with Mika, for some reason both cats decided to join us. Naturally they acted as if nothing had happened and they had been doing this all along. Mika refrained from chasing them, perhaps sensing the great privilege he was being subjected to. Then it became a daily ritual for all four animals: Mika, Tamaiti, *and* the older cats. Bliss. I was greedy, though. I kept hoping for more. I wanted the chooks and the bunny to come along, too.

When I began this project, I had no intention of transforming my older cats; they were not part of the experiment. But it gave me pleasure when they decided voluntarily to join us. It was a slow process, but something seemed to be happening to them. Megala lay down beside the rabbit's golden cage and rolled on his back and purred. He reached his paw into the cage and felt the rabbit. But when I brought Hohepa out, Megala hissed and struck at him, as he would have at another unknown cat. What, I wondered, was on his mind?

Moko had always seemed more like a feral cat than a domestic one. He was hyperalert to the slightest movement, the tiniest sound, seemingly always ready for flight. He walked like an animal still in the jungle, every sense alert. But even he seemed to be coming around. A few months into the project, he was on my bed one night when Tamaiti jumped on. Moko growled and hissed—and *stayed*! I realize that there is nothing magic about an older cat accepting a younger cat into his territory; still, Moko had been so adamant and clear about this whole idea leaving him cold (not to say disgusted) that to watch him begin to change his mind felt like a small miracle.

———

THE CHICKENS continued to enjoy the pleasures of the beach and seemed more comfortable there and with us every day. By now they were free to roam onto the beach, into the garden, or into our house. I wondered if they would ever satisfy my ambition for a walk with the dogs, cats, *and* chickens. Wasn't this a good example of my inability to be realistic? As far as I know, chickens did not go for walks on the beach with no purpose. (On the other hand, see how young Moana is strutting around the beach in the photo below.) They foraged, they searched for food, but they did not get pleasure just from walking. (Actually, when you think about it, neither do cats. But it's obvious they join me on my beach walks for the sheer pleasure of it.)

Yet the chickens were doing lots of things they would not do under natural conditions, like spending time with a rabbit. Moa and Moana had been together with Hohepa for longer than any of the other animals, since they shared the outdoor enclosure from the very start, and the three seemed to tolerate one

another's company well. The chickens would hop up onto one of the branches we put in there, and Hohepa would move to be under the branch. For a while, at least, there were no battles. Maybe this was because the rabbit was so inoffensive, demanding nothing, never asserting himself or fighting over food or space. I would sometimes find the chickens lying next to Hohepa, all three stretched out, comfortable, and contented, if not "happy." Nor did they seem to mind a dog and a cat (as we can see from the photo above of one of my assistants, Terese Storey, with Moa, Tamaiti, and Mika).

But the chickens continued to dislike the rats, pecking at them whenever they got the chance, even though the rats didn't harm the chickens in any way. Exposure seemed not to help.

Leila had disliked the rats, too; in fact, she abhorred them. Why? She has no idea. But once she came to know them, her feelings changed. Now she is a convert, with the fervor of all converts. She is always pressing the rats on reluctant guests. "Try holding them, you will like it," she says. And it often works. Sometimes all it takes for people who don't like rats is to come in close contact with them. Most people who dislike rats don't know why. Well, there is an easy answer: cultural conditioning and prejudice. In some countries—India, for example—this has not been the case. Does our abhorrence of rats stem from some inchoate memory of the plague hundreds of years ago? The fault, it turned out, lay with fleas, not rats; when the rats were killed, the fleas abandoned them and lodged on humans, thus causing the disease (which had been contained until then).

When I was a young Fulbright scholar studying Sanskrit in India, living in Calcutta, my friends tended to be pundits-in-training, rather orthodox Hindu religious types. One of the first places they took me to was Curzon Park in the heart of this enormous metropolis, where to my astonishment we saw a large enclosure with a small fence, no taller than a foot high, inside of which were thousands of wild rats running around in tunnels and mazes they had built for themselves in the earth. The rats could easily have escaped (rats can jump a foot-high fence and have the ability to climb anything), but they did not seem interested. We were with a young visitor from New York, who was horrified. "Rats!" she screamed, as if warning all of us away.

Manu, at only two, was terribly fond of the rats and wanted constantly to hold them. Oddly, they would stay quite still in his tiny hands, either because they were afraid of falling or because they recognized that he is just a child. I suspect it was the latter, since with me, they were far more active. When I let them loose on my desk (learning to live with small rat turds on my keyboard), they raced around but inevitably came back to me. They would climb up my shirt and perch on my shoulder, then race down my front to the desk again, and they could continue this for hours. At the beginning of our relationship, they would immediately hide, and I could barely coax them out. Now they didn't bother. Surely this meant they had learned from experience that there was nothing to fear. Where does "trust" come from in rats? In fact, what exactly *is* trust for a rat? Is it a thought?: I am safe. Or is it a feeling without cognitive content? Or is it a mood built out of knowledge *and* feeling?

It was still not easy for me to read the moods of the rats with anything like total accuracy. For example, how could I know when the rats were relaxed? Well, for one thing, they were not running away and hiding. Surely a frightened animal will try to put as much distance as possible between herself and the source of her fear. So if the rats didn't run away, I could take this to mean they were not frightened. The rats were at their *most* relaxed sitting in the hood of my workout sweatshirt and loved to be carried about like this. They liked it so much that if I called them when I was wearing the hood, they would come immediately, just like an obedient dog. Could I have imagined this?

Leila and I took the rats on a one-hour walk one day, holding them in our hands or putting them in the hood of my sweatshirt, when suddenly they both became agitated and obviously distressed, sniffing the air and exhibiting a look of panic on their faces. I could not figure it out. How do you ask a rat what's wrong? The rats were hard for me to figure out. They were also hard to let loose, because they wanted to run away. Well, actually they didn't want to run away, they just didn't want to be exposed. Exposure equaled danger to them, so we couldn't leave them to run around the lawn or even the picnic table on the beach. They wanted to and needed to be able to hide. That's why they love to dive into Leila's cleavage: It's the safest place around. (You can see Kia just emerging in the photo on page 84.) Visitors were sometimes shocked to see two small heads pop out from between Leila's breasts, the whiskers twitching nervously, bright little eyes alight with curiosity. Dark tunnels are their favorite hiding places (the insides of sleeves, for example). It seemed to me they also enjoyed being close to our bodies. It's odd that a rat wants to cuddle up next to a human, but it's true.

They did seem to get pleasure from being carried about and caressed. Kia, especially, loved it when I would hold her in one hand and then gently stroke her snout. She would go into ecstasies, lying immobile in my hand, closing her eyes, and making the strangest little sounds of contentment. But what if she really would have preferred to be somewhere else? How could I know? I think I found out.

Rats are nocturnal. They sleep most of the day and then

become wildly active at night. So it seemed unfair to leave them in their cage all night, even though it was a large cage. One night, I thought I would try allowing them to be free in my bedroom. For the first hour they were quiet. Then suddenly they came to life. It was like being in the middle of a rat circus. They were leaping from the windowsill to my chest and then making prodigious jumps from my chest back to the windowsill. I did not know they could jump so high. They were wildly excited. In and out of the covers, over my whole body, jumping, doing somersaults, having a great time. I did not sleep, of course. Finally, at three a.m. I had had enough. I put them back into their night cage, a much smaller version of the day cage (a bad reversal, I realize as I write this—it should have been the other way around; but the day cage was outdoors and the size of a small room and would not have fit inside our house). I put the cage into the bathroom, with the cage door open, so they could come and go, closed the bathroom door, and went to sleep.

In the morning I walked in and there was no sign of the rats. They had vanished. Finally I solved the mystery: The bidet that was in the bathroom had a pipe leading into the wall, and just above the pipe was a tiny hole that allowed access to the hollow inside of the bidet base, and they were ensconced inside that. I could feel their little noses, but for some reason they would not emerge. We tried everything—offering tasty tidbits of cheese, calling their names with a musical inflection—all with no success. A few hours later, some plaster fell out of the hole: They had bored into the wall and now had access to the whole of the inside skeleton of our house. I was sure we would never see them again. But that evening, a bit of strategically placed cheese brought them out and we were able to catch them and put them back in their cage. I felt like a traitor. It was now clear to me what rats wanted: *They wanted their freedom.* They liked us, no doubt, but more important to them was the ability to go where they pleased when they pleased. In other words, they were domesticated, but not entirely. This has been my experience with almost all domesticated animals: They are just a hairbreadth away from reverting to their wild ancestral state, and with good reason. How can we ever provide them with the advantages of the ecological niche in which they evolved? We cannot ever, it seems, improve on evolution.

But somewhere inside me still lurked the faint glimmer of hope that I was wrong—that we *could* improve on evolution. I say this because we humans seemed to have accomplished this with cats, who have a better deal living with us than they did living on their own. This is something I wrote about in *The Nine Emotional Lives of Cats,* theorizing that cats *chose* to be domesticated because of the pleasure they take in our company. They were designed to be solitary, and living with us, they must relinquish their solitude. But in return they get friendships across the species barrier. This is something they would *not* have achieved on their own and in their natural state never have. Whether they know it or not (and I have a sneaking suspicion they planned it that way), they cut a pretty good deal.

When I held the rats in my hand for a long time, I realized how easily they could be startled. Every sound, every sudden noise, made them twitch and become vigilant. They were ever alert to danger. Leila discovered that the rats hate any loud noise. One time they were inside her bosom when Ilan, quite a distance away from them, yelled at his brother, Manu. The rats startled. I did not know they had such good hearing. Once again it became clear to me that we had to start at the beginning with rats, rabbits, and chickens, slowly learning the sorts of things we seem to take for granted with dogs and cats. How well they hear, for example. We seem to know about dogs and how they see and hear because we are around them so much. Not so rats, rabbits, and chickens.

I had been studying the rats up close whenever they stood still long enough for me to do this. It never ceased to amaze me that we were so similar physically. I looked at Kia's front paws (she was so much more compliant than her sister Ora) and saw that she had four fingers (or were they toes?) with a vestigial fifth (thumb?). But the back paws had five long toes. Her diaphanous little ears were like human ears as well. Our similar physiology is one of the main reasons rats are used for experimental purposes. Well, as Darwin once wrote in his notebook (not about rats, but about animals in general): "Having proved men's and brutes' bodies of one type: almost superfluous to consider minds."* If they are so similar to us in their bodies, would not their minds (and by implication their feelings) be similar, too? It was the great issue he never addressed in any detail, but perhaps he believed future generations would discover the similarity there, too.

Strangely enough, any manual, for instance, *The Rat: An Owner's Guide to a Happy Healthy Pet* by Ginger Cardinal, will tell you about the "winning personality" of the rat and will describe rats as affectionate. *Rats* by Debbie Ducommun has a chapter entitled "Beginning Your Friendship." Yet "experts"— that is, animal science researchers—never discuss such issues.

Charles Darwin Notebooks, 1836–1844. Transcribed and edited by Paul H. Barrett et al. Cambridge, Mass.: Cornell University Press, 1987.

The popular new book by Robert Sullivan, *Rats: Observations on the History and Habitat of the City's Most Unwanted Inhabitants,* does not, of course, mention affection or friendship in the index. Yet rats clearly have the ability to feel it and the ability to induce it in others. I have seen ample proof of the latter. It was harder to gauge their capacity to feel affection for us. They seemed genuinely to want to be with us. When they *could* escape, or just get away from us, they didn't always do so. So it appeared that in some ways we had added to their repertoire rather than diminished their choices. We gave them pleasures different from, and other than, the ones they got from other rats. This was the only justification, it seemed to me, for confining them at all (my experiment notwithstanding), even to a cage newly enriched with bamboo leaves and branches, which they seemed to love. (We enriched the rats' cage in a new way each week: with rocks, sand, branches, bamboo, anything that would make their lives more exciting and interesting.)

The chickens were harder for me to read, at least initially, than the rats, probably because rats are mammals, like us, and birds are, well, different. I knew the chickens were fond of each other, for they could not bear to be apart. Both had a special plaintive call that they used the minute they were separated, even when I carried one outside and the other was waiting to be picked up next. "Where are you, where are you?" The meaning was clear; everybody who heard the sound understood what it meant. They obviously didn't mind being away from us, yet they also wanted to be in our presence. I learned this by closing the door on them, the door that leads from their enclosure to our living room. It drove them crazy, and they stood at the window and pecked and pecked until I gave in and let them inside. There was little for them to do inside (except poop, which they did with great gusto and exuberance)—and nothing to eat. I absolutely refused to strew our expensive hardwood floors with chicken feed. I could clean chicken poop off the floor, but once their sharp beaks pecked the wood, the scars would be there forever. If I left the door open, they would wander in and out, but mainly in. And if I closed it, they would immediately run up and demand to be let back in. Why? What was in it for them? If I could ask them, undoubtedly they would reply with something like "We just like it, that's all." Was this, then, how chickens showed affection? By remaining in our presence?

This raised an interesting question: Could I be certain that I was reading all the clues of friendship properly? Was I perhaps too human centered when I demanded gestures that I could easily interpret, such as approaching, cuddling, cooing, and other easily understood signs? In retrospect, I believe I may not have paid sufficient attention to something I call "watchful proximity." Watchful proximity is where one animal sits in the vicinity of another animal and appears to be doing nothing. "Appears" is the critical word here, for although it seems that way to us, in fact we may be missing the message entirely. Maybe just sitting and watching (Hohepa had mastered this skill to Zen perfection) *is* an eloquent message of acceptance. Perhaps far more is being communicated than we recognize.

(See the photo below of Mika and Hohepa in silent communication on the beach.) I am convinced now that this is indeed the case, that whenever two animals from a different species are in each other's presence and apparently doing nothing, they are saying the equivalent of "It's nice to be here with you."

Moa and Moana clearly thought it was nice to be here with me, although it could be that they would wait to come inside because they felt safer in the house and were looking for protection. On the beach, they continued to look to me as their protector. When the waves came up to their feet, they would run to me, and they would stay close to me whenever they heard a seagull or saw a dog. Was I a big chicken to them? Or was I just somehow, mysteriously, *protection*? Were they extending their sense of safety with me to inside the house because they didn't

make the same distinctions we do as to indoors and outdoors? When I left the house, they left with me. Was this because they felt affection, or was it that they felt protected? Of course, one does begin to feel affection for one's protector, even, as we have seen, in the extreme case of the "Stockholm syndrome," with someone who has been kidnapped. We have to face the fact that when we *force* dependency on animals, they are going to develop certain unnatural attachments. Yet for some reason our relationship seemed to me somewhat different from one of mere dependence—unnatural, perhaps, but pleasurable.

The chickens seemed to feel that I could also solve certain problems for them. Moana came running into the house from outside one afternoon, calling me: Moa, it turned out, was locked out of his enclosure. She was letting me know that I was to do something about it, and fast. It was amazing to see how badly even a chicken wants to communicate certain things. I could easily distinguish their distress calls from their happy sounds. They made wonderful sounds when they were in a good mood: soft little chuckles, a kind of humming to themselves. I loved to hear these unfamiliar and yet easy-to-decipher sounds. When Tamaiti charged them, they would make an annoyed sound. But when Megala charged, they would sound panicked. With good reason, it turned out.

I was on the beach, far from the house, when in spite of my increasingly bad hearing (like many men over sixty, I will *not* admit that I need a hearing aid), I thought I heard a distress call. I ran back to the house, and as I got closer, I realized both chickens were screaming (the only word for it). In the bushes at the side of the house, Megala had cornered Moa against the cedarwood and, when I arrived, was on top of him (by now we realized he was a rooster), looking, as it were, for the best way to begin his meal. I pulled Megala off and held Moa, who snuggled into my arm, peeping terrible sounds and shaking with fear. I thought he must have been injured, but it turned out that Megala had done nothing except frighten him. I felt so relieved. I also wondered, as disturbing as this encounter was, whether it signaled that Megala had learned some limits: He was not going to hurt one of his housemates, even if he was a bird. But I couldn't take any chances, alas; this just reminded me that I couldn't allow the chickens complete freedom as long as Megala was menacing them. Was there any chance that would ever change?

Megala soon showed me that his intentions were not benign. He was a menace to the rats as well. Leila was playing with Kia on the floor when out of nowhere Megala shot over, grabbed the rat in his mouth, and ran off. We were able to pry Kia out of his mouth, but Kia darted out of the house and into the garden, and then to our neighbor Raven's house, and we thought we might never see her again. Yet a few minutes later, Raven came over with Kia safe in her hand. Kia had run up to Raven, asking to be picked up. She had a puncture wound on her side, so Megala was not playing around this time. But it did not look serious, and a few hours later she was fine. And here is the most surprising thing: Immediately after, she did not appear frightened of Megala. Could it be that this was a strange kind of play? No, I was not that naive. I was convinced that Megala would have eaten that rat had we not been there. His look said clearly just that: "Give me that rat, give me that rat now, for dinner." (See the photo below of Robyn Haworth holding Kia and Megala.)

I WAS BEGINNING to learn what makes a chicken feel relaxed. Recently Moa and Moana were outside, lying down, when they extended their necks to their full length and laid them out on the grass, as if they were trying to reach something far away without moving their bodies. I realized with a start that they were happy and relaxed, but I had not known

that they took up this position when they felt so. Then they extended each wing in turn, and suddenly I saw that there were golden flecks in their feathers and that Moa, the male, had the beginnings of iridescent green feathers. They were beautiful. He also would lie down in the sun, stretch out one wing, then put his head flat on the ground and close his eyes. It was such a strange thing to see. But he would close his eyes for only a few seconds. The tiniest sound and he was wide awake. Chickens, I have now learned, have excellent hearing and even better vision. Nature equipped them well. Surprise, surprise, right? They seemed to enjoy it when I crouched to their eye level—that is, when I did not loom above them. This made sense, and I should have thought of it earlier. They often would lie down with their necks intertwined. Yes, they are birds!

That February (summer in New Zealand), unusually, there were gale-force winds. I could not take the chooks to the beach. I felt bad, as though I was letting them down. They kept coming up to the window facing into the kitchen and staring at me from their enclosure (which has windows into both our living room and the open kitchen). It was obvious that they wanted to go out and felt deprived. Well, they had a point. My goal was to make sure every day that they had the best life possible, but that was not always easy to provide. The fox in *The Little Prince* was right: We *are* responsible for whatever we tame, and that responsibility is enormous. How much easier to just admire wildlife, truly *wild* life.

———————

ONLY A FEW MONTHS after these seven "natural enemies" began to live in close contact, while they weren't yet best friends, they were one and all living peacefully together. At least it was so for the animals I had raised together. I considered that a significant accomplishment, the implications of which fascinated me. As for the older cats, I wasn't sure they would *ever* adjust or that it was even reasonable to expect them to.

As recently as the previous month, I would not have been able to include Hohepa the rabbit in our success story. Let loose, he just hopped away. The chickens didn't do that. Even the rats didn't. And of course, the dog and cat stayed close. But Hohepa was a loner, a solitary man who wants to do his own thing. Then, rather suddenly, things began to improve: I was able to set Hohepa free three days in a row, and he returned to his enclosure after several hours each time. It was my ideal: The chickens were out on the beach and lawn for the whole afternoon, and Hohepa was running around, mostly in the backyard of our neighbor Joan Chapple—which is, I confess, more interesting than ours (every imaginable plant grows there, but in such profusion that she does not mind letting Hohepa eat some)—returning to check on the rest of us from time to time, then hopping off. Tamaiti was playing with Mika the dog. The two older cats were lying contentedly nearby. We still had to figure out how the rats could be more fully included, but as Sir Patrick Bateson (the British imprinting expert) told me, hooded rats have been bred to be docile and friendly, and with Ora and Kia, the breeding definitely succeeded. "Look," he said when he was inspecting my project, "how easygoing they are." He took great pleasure in them.

They were still wary of the other animals, even those not committed to eating them: Tamaiti, Mika, and Hohepa. I may have missed what was not obvious, though. Later developments suggest this as the likely explanation.

————— ❋ —————

THE PEACEABLE
KINGDOM

TO SOME EXTENT, I can say that after six months the goal of this experiment was achieved: All the animals tolerated one another, and none was aggressive with any of the others. This was precisely what I had been hoping to demonstrate—that if animals (humans?) are raised together in proximity, and if they have a "caretaker" ("leader" is too grandiose a word, especially for me) dedicated to achieving tolerance and a peaceful environment, the animals (humans?) will move naturally in this direction. It is not something that needs to be forced upon them, it will simply happen. I was satisfied that what I saw with my own eyes verified this belief and that the animals bore this out.

The next step was to see if the animals would become friends, but I decided to adjust my goal: It was no longer a question of creating friendship once the peaceable kingdom was achieved, but rather a matter of giving the animals freedom, the freedom I included in the definition of happiness, human or otherwise. After all, I began to reason, what I wished for these animals (or any other animal, for that matter) was happiness. So I still had to ask myself, were all the animals leading an optimally happy life? Here is where the animals have ended up:

Moa and Moana, the chickens, were now free: In principle, they could stay out all day long. And they did indeed roam the beach, use our garden, play in the grass, but mostly, if we were indoors, they wanted to be indoors with us. If I was inside and closed the door, the chickens would stand mournfully by the window staring in, like orphans at a Christmas dinner. I couldn't stand it, so I let them in.

I made a deal with the neighbors: I would keep the chickens in until eight a.m. every morning on weekdays and until nine on weekends. Otherwise, Moa's crowing at five forty-five every morning bothered them. (I loved the sound at any time—it always made me feel I was in the country and that all was well with the world.)

The chickens decided the warm laundry room was their favorite place to sleep. They had wandered in there one day, and they flew up into one of the cubbyholes and settled down for the night. We put straw into the cubby in the evening after that, and every day, as soon as the sky began to darken, they headed for the laundry room from wherever they were—the garden, the beach, or more usually in our house. And every morning at eight I took them out to the beach, even though they would follow me straight back into the house (or if I was sitting reading on the deck, they would follow me there and hang out until I returned to the house). I think they saw me as part of their flock, an über-chicken, so where I went, they went. At first I stayed out with them on the beach, but I discovered that they were fine on their own and that I was being an over-protective mother. Also at first I did not let them back in the house, but they looked so determined at the door; they simply would not give up. They would wait patiently until I weakened and let them in. I liked their look of contentment more than I hated their messiness.

Mika seemed to have a happy life, but there was a new rule in Auckland: a US$300 fine if a dog was caught off leash. This draconian law was enacted because not long ago there had been several tragic maulings of small children by dogs. The dogs were fighting dogs, which are illegal here and everywhere. I firmly believe that when a dog is vicious, you must look to the humans with whom he or she lives. Even though our house is on the beach and in a secluded area, it is considered to be in Auckland proper—after all, we are only fifteen minutes from the central business district. But it would be unlikely, unless somebody complained, that any dog warden would come down here. So all the dogs on the beach—four at the moment—were still off leash. Mika was getting to the age, almost a year old, where for at least a good part of the day she wanted to lie around on our deck, absorbing the sunshine and playing with her new best friend, Bella, a dog who recently moved onto the beach. Mika would go for many walks a day with us, and we took her just about everywhere we went. She was never bored, for there were always visitors, both human and canine. She had another good friend, Missy, the dog who lives with Robyn Haworth. Robyn's daughter was one of the volunteers, and her family had said they would be happy to have Mika come over for a few hours in the evening if we went out. This worked beautifully: She went on play dates when we went to the movies. More people should exchange play dates for their dogs.

Seeing Mika interact with the other animals, and other dogs especially, I realized that we were still at the beginning of our knowledge of these extraordinary beings, so like us, yet so different (in most respects better, I am ashamed to say—ashamed, that is, for my species). There was always more to learn and more to observe. Watching Mika take such immediate interest in another animal (dogs are truly subject to the proverbial *coup de foudre* as much as humans are), I realized that in my book *Dogs Never Lie About Love* I neglected to mention something else that almost all dogs share with some humans: love at first sight. They don't need to think about it, mull it over, compare, worry about commitment; they know immediately: It's either yes or no. What do they know? How can they tell so quickly and so unerringly? Is it the look, the smell, the body language, or something we fail to recognize altogether? The latter, I will bet.

As for Tamaiti the cat, well, down here on our beach you need not confine a cat, of course, and nobody would ask you to.

So Tamaiti was free to go wherever he pleased day and night. Being a rag doll, he wanted primarily to stay around us. He loved going for long walks with us on the beach, and his friendship with Hohepa the rabbit was getting deeper by the day. They would frolic and play and chase each other for hours every day. Most people who dropped by and learned about "the experiment" hinted that they would be willing to take Tamaiti when I finished writing this book. You could not meet him and not like him. He had no enemies among animals or people. When Tamaiti played with the rats, which he did often, we noticed that he kept his claws in. He avoided hurting them, and they knew they could trust him. (You can see from the photo below that even when he was getting acquainted he was gentle with Kia.) From the day we got him, he never hunted. I could not

know if this was because he had taken in the main lesson of tolerance from this experiment or because he was the kind of cat who would never have hunted in any event. Rag dolls, as a breed, certainly do not hunt as intensely or as often as other cat breeds, but they do hunt. Tamaiti was like Ferdinand the bull: He would rather smell the flowers, thank you very much.

For a while, Hohepa the rabbit had the perfect life for a rabbit. Early in the morning, we would open his enclosure and he would hop out to spend the day wandering from garden to garden and house to house. Now you see him, now you don't. As soon as it got dark, he would wander back into his enclosure; we would feed him, and he would wait patiently for the morning and his renewed freedom. It was bliss. Then the neighbors started to complain: He was eating their gardens. They tried fencing them off, but Hohepa would dig his way under the fence and decimate their greenery. I could understand their annoyance. Worst of all, they were afraid the dogs would gang up, chase Hohepa, and tear him to pieces. Could I guarantee that would not happen? I could not. So reluctantly I agreed to keep Hohepa in his enclosure and allow him out only for supervised play on the grass. He was miserable: He kept staring out the door that had previously always been open for him. We let him wander through the house, but his only interest in the house was the front door and when it might open to let him out. Manu inadvertently did open the door for him occasionally, and Hohepa actually escaped three times. The situation was not ideal. But what would be an ideal situation for him?

Clearly, Hohepa relished his freedom to roam more than anything else. If I could have found a home that would have allowed him to wander all day, I would have let him go, even though it meant breaking up the peaceable kingdom and depriving Tamaiti of a best friend. (You can see how happy they are together resting in the enclosure.) Hohepa's happiness mattered more than my experiment. But where would I find such a place? In England and in America, there are "eccentrics" who devote their lives to rabbits. They fence off acres of land, making it safe for rabbits. While there are no natural predators of rabbits in New Zealand, there were also no such people in New Zealand. Or at least if there were, I had never heard of them. But I put the word out with the animal rights organization SAFE (Save Animals from Exploitation), and perhaps such an enlightened being would appear sooner or later.

We had a scare with Hohepa recently. He was missing for

two days, and we were all anxious that something terrible had happened to him. My friend Gary, the former head of SAFE in Auckland, was playing with Manu on the trampoline (which is set into the ground so that children cannot fall off) when suddenly he felt an inverse bouncing movement from inside the hole underneath the trampoline. "Someone or something was bouncing up as I was bouncing down, thumping against my feet as I landed," he told me. Of course, it was none other than Hohepa, who had fallen down into the four-foot hole under the trampoline and could not climb out. He was, I fancied, unusually affectionate for the next few hours, nuzzling us and lying contentedly in our laps. Usually he did not pay much attention to us, and it is hard to feel a connection with somebody who appears indifferent to you. Respect, yes, but not friendship. I felt I had failed to see "the person inside" Hohepa, his distinct personality. The problem could have been me, or it could been that Hohepa had so little interest in me that I missed what might have been obvious to somebody else. The scare made me realize, though, how important to us he had become and that perhaps he was not as indifferent as appearances suggested.

I was concerned about Kia and Ora as well. I would have loved for them to be free all evening or all night and confined to their cages only during the day, when they seemed to sleep in any event. But how could I do this? I could not give them the free run of the house. We had too many cats; moreover, it was a large house and we might never have found them again.

So I compromised: From about six p.m. until late in the evening, I kept them with us; they watched TV and wandered about the room. Before I went to sleep, I would read in the bedroom and allow them to leap from my chest to the windowsill (about two feet away) and back again; this seemed to be their favorite game. Then around ten p.m. I would put them in a small indoor cage, to protect them from the winter cold of their huge cage outside. But they were miserable there. From ten until morning I could hear them going crazy, climbing the cage and desperately seeking a way out. I knew how badly they wanted to explore and wander, yet I couldn't figure out a way to make this possible. I didn't think there was a good solution, and I was beginning to think that people should not keep rats, unless, like Rachel Rosenthal, the wonderful French performance artist living in Los Angeles, they give them the full range of their home. Her whole home was a rat city, as she describes in her charming book about the main rat in her life, *Tatti Wattles: A Love Story.*

I e-mailed Rachel Rosenthal, thinking she might have some advice for me. Her answer gave me a scare. She told me to watch out for rat teeth, about how they grow and grow and eventually go right through the palate. So I looked at Kia and Ora while we were taking them on a walk, and I became alarmed at how long their teeth looked. I rushed to the vet, but he calmed me down, telling me it was unusual for teeth to grow so large unless we were not giving them hard things to eat, which of course we are. The trick was to think about how they would live in the wild, what they would do, what they would eat, and then try to duplicate those natural conditions as far as possible.

Keeping this principle in mind, we finally found what seemed like an ideal solution for the rats. It came about because Leila had fallen in love with Kia (and equally with Ora, she told me, although Ora is more timid). I did not entirely understand this development. Leila had never been an "animal person" (that is, somebody who has loved animals from early childhood). If anything, I had assumed Leila would bond with Mika or Tamaiti. The rats seemed an unlikely possibility. But then who understands love? I asked her for an explanation, but she refused to give me one. "It just happened," was her comment. I think something about their vulnerability got to her. Also, perhaps the fact that they loved to go for rides ensconced in her bosom somehow appealed to her. They trusted her, and she did not let them down.

We let them stay (mostly asleep) in their large cage during the day. But when visitors came, which happened several times a day, the children among them were drawn immediately to the rat cage, and out they came for fun and games. We also took them out to play at various points during the day whenever we thought they might be bored (rats show you they are bored by climbing the wires of the cage and almost literally "begging" to be taken out). At night we would take them into the bedroom, in a smaller cage, and leave it open. They then had the freedom of the whole large room, and especially the bed, which they loved. They would run over our faces all night; at first this was hard to get used to, but soon we could just about sleep. They loved the freedom and roamed constantly from cage to bed to the huge wardrobe with all its hiding spots.

The only problem was that while Kia would be ready to come back in the morning, Ora hid. For days we would see her only at night, when she emerged to play. We left food out for her, but I couldn't help wondering where she was leaving her droppings and where she peed. Kia, oddly, would go back into her cage to go to the bathroom, and when she finished she would reemerge. Who would have thought a rat could be so fastidious? Come to think of it, Kia almost never peed or defecated when she was on our person. When we put her on a table, she would do her business, but never on us. This was more than cleanliness; it struck me that she was being thoughtful, that she somehow recognized we would not like it. I asked other rat lovers about this, and I heard the same story: Rats are considerate. That was the adjective that sprang to mind most often. Amazing, isn't it, that the word *considerate* should be applied to rats? It is undoubtedly deserved and much used by rat lovers. And actually, in our neighborhood, there are more and more rat enthusiasts: We seem to have started a trend. Children who came to our house and met the rats have begged their parents for one, and several friends have reluctantly given in. The children are delighted with their new companions.

Six months into the project, I was relieved to observe that the chickens no longer needed me to protect them. Moa had

become the big macho protector of Moana. He was a large rooster now, and woe to the dog or cat who took him on. He would
come out flying, talons at the ready. Everybody would back off,
and he would strut off, cackling proudly. When Bella, the new
dog on the block, came racing at Moana, she found herself faced
with an enraged rooster flying straight at her face. She took off
in the opposite direction like a bullet! Moa strutted away,
clucking softly to himself: "That's right—I'm the new boss
around here."

The one time this did not work was when Bella—looking so
much like a fox that some people actually thought she might be
one; she certainly behaves like one when it comes to chickens—
suddenly made a mad dash for Moana and caught her in her
mouth. Alerted by the screams of the hen, Leila came running
out of the house, caught Bella by her tail just as she was trying
to disappear under the house, and pulled her out. I came rush-
ing from my office just in time to see Moana emerge from
Bella's mouth, missing some feathers for sure but otherwise not
harmed. Moa looked crestfallen, as if he had let down his mate
in a crucial moment. He had. Perhaps he was as taken by surprise as the rest of us. From this we learned that some dogs simply can't be trusted around chickens.

Now that we had our peaceable kingdom, there were things
we could do that we could not consider before. One of the dis-
advantages of having so many animals was that we could not
travel. Well, we solved that one.

The Volvo station wagon was sluggish. Understandable.

Inside were Leila and me, Manu, Ilan, Ilan's friend Sophia, and all our luggage. Plus Moa and Moana, Kia and Ora, Mika, and Tamaiti, not to mention assorted cages, food, water bottles, and endless toys for children and animals alike. (Only Hohepa was staying behind, with Raven, as we were not sure how he would take to a new environment and we had nothing large enough in which to keep him confined there.)

It was a strange sight. "Are those chooks you have in there?" people asked at our first rest stop. The dog, the cat, and the rats were all free to roam around the car; the chooks were in a cat carrier. We were heading for our house in the Coromandel. We had bought a small craftsman's house and a little cottage on the river the year before, on five acres with gardens, trees, and native bush. I thought nobody could appreciate this beautiful spot more than I did. I was wrong: The chickens liked it even more. Actually, it was strange to see how Mika, Tamaiti, and the chickens seemed to fit into the landscape better than we did, perhaps because this was an even more natural environment than our beach house. They were right at home, immediately.

A friend had fixed up an old chicken coop for the chooks. We put them in, but they were clearly frightened and disappeared under the house. Our neighbor wandered over to tell us that there were stoats (a weasel-like animal, introduced into New Zealand a few hundred years ago by Western settlers, that causes havoc among native birds because they did not evolve to avoid such a predator) in the garden who would make short work of the chooks that night. I tried to coax them out but was unsuccessful. They huddled under the house in a place we could not reach. We sent little Manu, who was two and small, underneath, and he was able to reach them, but he didn't know what to do with them once he got there. I couldn't sleep that night; I kept waiting for the screams of Moa in the jaws of a stoat. At five forty-five, I was relieved to hear Moa's morning crow. But we still could not get them out. The children had the idea of seeding the steps of the little ladder into the chicken coop. It worked. Soon they were out in the front garden, then on the porch. That night I put them in the carrying cage and kept them inside the house.

Had it not been for the stoats, the chooks would have been safe outdoors. They had been fantastic travelers: not a peep out of them. The rats, on the other hand, were nervous, perhaps because they were used to a huge cage and we had taken them in a smaller, temporary cage. The kids enriched the cage with tunnels, branches, rocks, and the like, and that made an immediate difference.

It was a wonderful two days. We took many walks in the hills above our property, and Mika and Tamaiti came on all of them. The chickens lay in the sun on the grass in front of the river, completely at ease. At night we allowed the rats to run free in the bedroom, since there were no enemies about, and they loved it. The trip back was uneventful, as if the animals were now seasoned travelers. The chickens made not a sound; the rats slept in our sleeves. Mika had her head out the window, sniffing the world; the cat moved from lap to lap. I was pleased to realize that we could travel in this way whenever we wished, something I would not have thought possible before.

THE REAL SURPRISE of the experiment, and the unexpected success for me, was what had been happening to the two older cats, Moko and Megala. Against all expectations, and contrary to all rules of cat behavior and their own evolution, the two older, semiferal cats had not only accepted the younger animals, they had also stopped hunting! Megala was now getting along fine even with the chickens—he was amiable and exhibited a live-and-let-live philosophy. He would close his eyes when they were pecking away at the ground nearby, as if he were bored, indifferent, or accepting. He was this way with all the animals except the rats. I guess his behavior with the rats was something so hardwired that it was outside his control. He knew that when we were holding the rats, he could not harm them, and he would then extend a paw tentatively to touch them. He liked to touch noses with them, too. He no longer made any move, as he had in the beginning, to snatch them away. However, when we left Kia on the kitchen counter one day (believing in Megala's complete conversion), Megala noticed and was on her in a flash. He leapt down with Kia squealing in his mouth. Luckily I was right there and was able to rescue Kia. The surprise to me was that she had no teeth marks on her. Megala may have intended to eat her, but at least he was not shredding her immediately, as he might have done earlier.

About six months after we began this experiment, Moko too began to leave the chickens alone. I realized this during a visit from Sir Patrick Bateson, the British academic and expert on animal behavior. As I walked him back up the hill from the beach to the road, I inadvertently left the chickens imprisoned in their golden cage. When I returned, there were Moko and Megala sitting next to the cage, which they can hop into easily, washing themselves nonchalantly as if butter would not melt in their mouths. The chickens were within, unharmed.

I can easily understand why Tamaiti did not hunt birds or rats: He'd been raised with them. His instincts had been subverted at the earliest age. One day he "caught" (if that is the right word) a baby mouse and looked positively mortified when I removed the little guy. He looked at me with genuine surprise, as if to say, "I was just playing with him; I wouldn't have hurt him." This is probably true, but since the mouse was very small, I could not take the chance of finding out if he was as good as his word.

But it was hard to understand why both older cats suddenly gave up hunting at the age of three. It had been at least two or three months since they had brought in a bird, a rat, or even a gecko, all of whom had appeared with heartbreaking regularity in the past. I could not explain it. But I could speculate: Might it be that having realized *these* animals were off-limits, *these* birds (Moa and Moana), *these* rats (Kia and Ora), they somehow generalized to *those* birds, *those* rodents—in other words, to other animals *in general*? If so, it would be a most remarkable phenomenon. I am not putting it beyond the bounds of possibility, but of course I realized that hunting could resume any day. Meanwhile, I was keeping my philosophical fingers crossed.

This lapse (whether permanent or temporary) in hunting fascinated me and everyone else I told about it. I asked friends with cats if they had ever seen anything like it. Nobody had. Much older cats sometimes stop hunting simply because they can't manage it any longer. But I encountered no case of a healthy cat in the prime of life who "decides" to give up hunting. I understand the temerity of using the word *decide* in this case, but I don't know how else to account for it.

It is possible that I have omitted something in trying to explain this mystery. For example, could Moko and Megala have simply lacked the motivation to hunt, being so well fed? This was unlikely, since they were eating the same way they had over the previous three years, when both had been mighty hunters. I should also add that three of their former housemates, the cats I raised together with them from kittenhood, now lived elsewhere and continued to hunt. Two were with my mother up the road. One lived with a neighbor, and he too continued to hunt. There were still birds and rats and geckos in the vicinity of our house and on the beach that my two cats could easily have hunted. They didn't. I am afraid (actually I am

FOUR

※

TRANSFORMATIONS

WHAT HAD I ACHIEVED in raising the peaceable kingdom? The achievements lie in a simple piece of human (or at least my own, as if we humans could improve on nature) hubris: I believe enforced contact has something to recommend it. It is a little like an enforced vacation or pushing a student to attend college. There is nothing genetic going on during a vacation or in going to college. We do it because we have to, sometimes. And we often do it reluctantly. Then we expand: first our horizons, then our views, and ultimately our lives. We are enriched. Here is the riddle: Suppose we force something on another person, but he or she ultimately benefits? Raising a child makes me keenly aware of this dilemma: It is not in a two-year-old's immediate interest to sit in a car seat or to wear a helmet when he rides his speedy little scooter. But he does because we make him do so, because we know it is ultimately in his interest even if he does not know it. Now how about expanding his world? That is what school is all about. If it were up to him, well, "No thanks, I prefer to do without expansion."

We have had one tragedy. I am grateful that it was only one, for I feared constantly for the lives of many of the animals living here, simply because of the world we live in. Ora died or was killed on June 23, 2004. She got out of her cage downstairs in the evening. I was sure we would find her easily before we went to sleep. We did not. Before we got into bed, Leila said, "Let's put Megala out for the night." She feared that the older cat would harm Ora. I must make a mental note, yet again, never to question Leila; she is always right. But it was a cold winter night and I was reluctant, certain that Megala would not find Ora or, if he did, would not harm her. After all, he was a changed cat, right? In the morning I went down to my computer, and there at the foot of my desk was Ora, stiff with death, with Megala sniffing her. He looked up at me, all innocence: "I walked into your office, and here is what I found." Too much of a coincidence to believe. I would like to think she died of natural causes. True, she had been getting thinner every day for reasons I could not explain. Also, no marks of any kind were visible on her small body. There was a live socket right next to my desk, and it is possible that Ora, in trying to get up, put her tiny paw into it to get a purchase and was electrocuted.

When Ilan woke at seven a.m., his first question was, "Did you find Ora?" I was tempted to lie to him. Then I realized he had the right to know what had happened to his little friend.

After all, it was a true friendship, each making concessions to the other. Ilan was inconsolable. Even two-year-old Manu was crying (as were Leila and I), and he kept calling out, "Ora, Ora!" It was a terrible feeling to lose a small, helpless animal you have loved. It may seem odd to others to use the word *love* when talking about a rat, but to those who knew her, there was nothing to feel ashamed about in having such affection for the tiny "person" (I should not have to use quotation marks) inside this little rat.

We buried her in the garden, under an olive tree; Ilan put fresh flowers on her grave and sat there by himself for a long time before we convinced him to leave for school. He shared the story of her life and death with his friends at school, I heard later, and not one child thought of making fun of him or Ora. Her life was brief but happy. Nor was it in vain: She taught at least one little boy that love crosses the species barrier with remarkable ease. I have a feeling this lesson will last Ilan a lifetime.

Later that day, I thought about Ora's last moments—how, if Megala had killed her, she would have sensed the cat's approach. I pictured her panicked attempt to escape, the horror as the claws closed on her. She had obviously been looking for me at my desk, since I found her right next to my wastebasket under the desk where my feet normally are. Would she have thought of us at that moment—willing us to appear and save her from certain death? I was left with a bunch of *if onlys*. If only I had listened to Leila and let Megala out for the night. If only I had searched for Ora more thoroughly before going to bed. If only Megala had better learned his lesson for the peaceable kingdom. But then perhaps he had; perhaps Ora died from an electric shock. Either way it is sad, for her life was only half-over. Was Kia forlorn at the death of her sister? We could not tell. I am not sure how rats exhibit despondency.

Sometimes I think rats have been domesticated so successfully that they have lost all natural fear, that maybe Ora was not aware of the danger Megala posed. But it is not so. I was playing with Kia on my desk the day after Ora was killed, holding her tiny paws between my fingers, when suddenly she became hyperalert. I noticed nothing unusual. In the next second, she was off like a small rocket. She ran to the other side of the room at a speed I had never seen her use before. She was clearly terrified. I turned around and there was Megala in hunting mode (even if it was only a memory of his former days), crawling forward on his belly. Kia had never done this before. Did she know what Megala might have done to her sister? She made no sound, but she was panicked just the same. Either she always knew about Megala or something had alerted her to his untrustworthiness. (Speaking of sounds, I almost never hear Kia make a sound. But when I accidentally stepped on her tail after her encounter with Megala, she let out a small but distinctive yelp. It was the first time I had heard her "speak.")

I had been told that rats do not welcome strange rats into their colony and that even a single rat will fight to the death with any introduced rat. Not Kia. Feeling that she must be lonely without Ora, we brought home a young female rat who had been born to a friend of ours. Kia nuzzled her instantly, and that very night they slept in a tight rat ball. Since then they have become inseparable. Ilan was allowed to name the newcomer, so her name is Stuart (from *Stuart Little*). I knew Kia was a gentle rat, and I knew that she would not harm a baby rat no matter what the experts said, and I was right. You cannot always believe accepted wisdom.

Kia's gentleness could perhaps be explained partly by the enormous amount of human (and other) contact she has had. We just spent three whole days with her outside of her cage. We went up to the Coromandel and decided not to bring any cage for Kia; instead we carried her about during the day in our sleeve or coat pocket or shirt pocket, and at night we let her roam the house. She always wound up in our bed, curled at our feet (I think it is warmest there). Since the only other animal sharing the house at the time was Tamaiti, there was no chance Kia would come to any harm. I was a bit concerned that she might simply walk away, but she didn't. She stuck fairly close to us. I would have loved to take her for a walk the way we took the cats for a walk—that is, with her following along on the ground. But given her size, this would have been difficult, and I worried that if she did disappear, even if by mistake, we might not be able to find her again. It was too big a risk.

I had learned to value the happy life and the free life for animals above all other values. I suppose it is the same for humans. In order to achieve this, I needed to do what I had done a few

months ago—free myself from the valuable but perhaps ideal-
istic goal of creating soul mates. The surprise you will learn
about in a few minutes is that I need not have fenced myself in
that way.

There could be no doubt that all the animals who lived
with us now would have lived very different lives on their
own. All except the chickens had come to not only tolerate
but also accept one another. Why would they not, you might
ask, given that all their needs were met: shelter and all the
food they might need or want? Because instinctually they are
not equipped to accept "enemies" as "friends." Except that
they clearly have. We are increasingly aware of how plastic
instinct is, of how it responds to experience and even to exter-
nal pressure. Here I have gotten to see that plasticity at work
close up. I was prepared for this result. It was what I had
hoped to achieve. But I hoped for more. I wanted to know
what it would take to cause a true transformation of the very
being of the animal.

When I was a graduate student studying Buddhist texts in
Sanskrit, I came across an expression, actually a single Sanskrit
word, that made a deep impression on me. The word was
ashrayaparavrtti, which means something like a complete turning over of the ground you are standing on. *Ashraya* refers to
your stance, your home ground, the place where you are
grounded. *Paravrtti* means it has been turned upside down, it
has been transformed. The Buddhists use the term to refer to
somebody whose worldview is suddenly transmuted in a single

moment, a kind of conversion to the blinding truths of Buddhism. Was this sort of transformation possible in the case of my animals? I did not want to admit to this goal, because I did not want to be disappointed, although I fully expected to be. I was not.

In this book, Hohepa the rabbit has sometimes received short shrift. I expected the least from him and the chickens, I suppose, and at the beginning he alone lived up (or down) to those diminished expectations. As I have written, he seemed uninterested in us and in the other animals. He waited for his opportunity to escape, and when he found it he would leave his enclosure and disappear for days. True, he always came back (that should have been the first hint that he was hardly a wild animal), but as soon as he could, he would leave again. It was only a matter of time, we assumed, before he would leave for good.

We tried to tie him to us and to the other animals, sometimes literally. Ilan, for example, took to carrying Hohepa around in a sling, just as one carries a small baby. (You can see the photo of this lovely arrangement on page 122.) It gave Ilan great pleasure and also pleased everyone else who saw us walking in this way. But it seemed to make little impression on Hohepa himself. I felt he was always supremely indifferent to us and to the other animals. We would put Hohepa, the chickens, the kitten, and even the rats in the enclosure and leave them be for hours, but he showed no interest in any of the other animals. Or so it seemed to us.

We were wrong. One day, Hohepa was transformed: Suddenly he *wanted* to be part of the gang. He would hang around, run outside, and come back a few moments later; he would walk on the beach and return; he would go to neighboring houses (avoiding their gardens, it would seem, for they no longer complained of nibbled lettuces!) and stay just a few minutes, lest he miss anything exciting. He would wait for the evening so that he could accompany us on our night adventures, when we would go exploring the beach in the moonlight. "This is my home now," he seemed to be saying. The reason? Simple: He had fallen in love with Tamaiti. It seemed to be mutual, for they were now inseparable. One day soon after this transformation, I walked into the den where we watch videos, and there on the little footstool was Hohepa, sound asleep. Next to him, with his paw resting casually about Hohepa's shoulders, was Tamaiti. (Below, you can see the picture I took at the time.)

So we *did* reach goal number four, the one I thought only a chimera: Two of the animals had become best friends. There was no coercion—not physical, in any event. But we did set up the conditions that made it possible, that gave them the opportunity to be together, something that would not have happened in the wild. We kept Hohepa in places where he was bound to see Tamaiti, since Tamaiti spent a great deal of time in the enclosure. We would often put Hohepa in the golden cage next to the spot where Tamaiti was sunning himself. He was around the other animals as well, but for reasons known only to him-

self, it was Tamaiti he chose to bond with. Tamaiti, too, had ample opportunity to befriend any of the other animals and was on good terms with all of them, but he chose to be this close only to Hohepa. It was a mutual choice. Of course, we were always rooting for something like this to happen. But they took the opportunity and ran with it. And they did it in their own time, not according to our schedule. The needs of my experiment never weighed heavily on its protagonists.

One night, by the light of a full moon, I called Mika and we set out for a walk on the beach. It was the middle of winter, but a mild night. The tide was high, and we could see and hear the lapping of the waves on the sands. As usual, I called for the cats, and in a few minutes I could see their little shapes running from the house to join us for this late night walk. It was the best time for them, for no other people or animals were around, and I think they felt at their safest. I turned around, and where I expected only the three cats, Moko, Megala, and Tamaiti, I saw a fourth ghostly figure following close behind the last cat: Hohepa was hopping along, eager to catch up with Tamaiti and the rest of us. He wanted to join the procession, and he did. Radical transformation, a fundamental change in an animal of whom one does not expect it—that was the gift I was given by my "experiment." Two best friends from different species whose greatest pleasure was to walk along a deserted beach at midnight.

Both Moa and Moana were becoming more tolerant of us. It was no longer hard to catch them. They allowed us to pick them up. The kids loved to do it, and the chooks certainly tolerated it. I could not tell, though, whether they got pleasure from being held and carried. I was hoping that one day they would fly into my lap and demand to be stroked and utter those lovely little sounds of pleasure they often gave each other. But so far this had not happened (but see below a photo of them sitting fairly contented in my lap). Strangely, they still rarely left the inside of the house. This was where they preferred to be, and even the front yard and garden did not tempt them for long. They liked to be around us, but I am not sure that had as much to do with affection as with feelings of safety and familiarity.

But with the other animals, they were holy terrors. Moa attacked the cats whenever he saw them. He did the same to Hohepa and Kia. Not to Mika, though; perhaps she was too big, or was it that she had never represented a threat? In fact, both Moa and Moana chased all the other animals with the exception of Mika. They would not tolerate the cats anywhere near them, or the rabbit, and least of all Kia the rat. I had heard them described as "brats" by visiting children who had difficult siblings (and hence direct experience in such matters). I could not entirely disagree, though I found the chooks compelling nonetheless. Leila did not, and she wondered what I saw in them. Well, it is always difficult to explain attachment. I loved to watch their true nature as wild birds come to the fore. I liked the sounds they made, especially those of pleasurable contentment. I liked their stubbornness: They would wait for hours outside the house in order to get in for God knows what purpose. I also took pleasure in their commitment to each other, how they were always together, and how unhappy a brief separation made them. I guess most of all I reveled in the "chickenness" of these chickens.

Why hadn't they bonded with the other animals? Their reticence couldn't have been due to the fact that they were birds or that birds are simply more timid around large animals. For how Mika and Fuzzbucket, the magpie from next door, played! The bird would grab Mika's tail and try to hop away with it. Delighted, Mika would watch intently, then get down close to the ground and crawl to Fuzzbucket, making the strangest play sounds I had ever heard, pleading to play. She was positively possessed. Fuzzbucket would wait, then leap into the air and land on the other side of Mika. Mika would throw herself onto her back and try to catch the bird in her paws, as if Mika were a cat. Fuzzbucket knew it was a game, and one she could win, too. They would play like this for a long time. The neighbors were enchanted. Who would not be? So even if my chickens hadn't achieved all I would have liked in our little peaceable kingdom, we at least had a bird in the neighborhood eager to join and participate in our interspecies fun.

I learned that the first year was a period of transition and that it was too early to say what would happen. It takes time for the bonds of friendship to grow. Who would have expected that Hohepa would turn out to be the animal to form an intense attachment with another animal? When you are watching closely, three months might seem like a long time, but in the scheme of things it is as nothing. If we hesitated to say that Hohepa was in love, we could say he was infatuated, for he would spend all his time waiting for Tamaiti and when he saw him would rush over to greet him. Groom him. Kiss him (or were they little love bites?). Dote on him. And during the late night walks with the three cats, Mika and Hohepa hopping right alongside us had become routine. When we carried the rats, that left only the chickens as the holdout.

Hohepa was a typical rabbit—skittish, nervous about play with other animals, not at all bonded to us, eager to run off by himself. For the longest time, he would have little to do with us. Only very slowly did he allow us to stroke him, and it took even longer for him to allow us to pick him up. What was it that might have taken place in his mind as he changed and began to wish to be with us and with the other animals? Did he ever think about it? "Well, I guess I was wrong, this *can* be fun. Maybe I was just prejudiced." How common is this sort of transformation among rabbits? Most people I spoke to who live with rabbits told me that their rabbits were either very friendly right away or they weren't; it was a matter of temperament, and they didn't undergo major changes over a few months. So our experience seems not to have been typical. On the other hand, perhaps Hohepa was simply biding his time, getting to know us and the other denizens of our community. He could just have been slow. Besides, trust takes time to build. He had to overcome his unpleasant beginning in a dirty cage with many other rabbits, then the trauma of being crushed by a dog kennel. And truth be told, probably few rabbits have ever been offered the chance to make this sort of transformation in the first place, so we may never know how many were capable of it and were simply awaiting the opportunity.

As with any other animal, I am not certain to what extent "breed" makes any difference to how affectionate a rabbit is. I was told that Flemish giants were notoriously friendly and docile. Well, Hohepa was certainly docile, but it took him a long time to become friendly. Some of the mini lop-eared rabbits have a reputation for being standoffish, but I have known a few who were instantly friendly with people and other animals in a household. Upon what does it depend? I am afraid nobody knows the answer.

This sort of transformation happens all the time in the case of feral cats, or at least has been happening from the time people have become aware of the ability to transform a feral cat into a domestic one. This is a relatively new concept (only within the last ten years, I believe). Previously, it was thought that if a cat was born feral, or even forced to go feral because of circumstances, nothing could be done to reverse the process. Once feral, always feral. I certainly believed this, and when I inherited a house with a feral cat in the yard, nothing I did seemed to change him. I was patient for months, and that cat would not come near me. But this need not be so, it turns out. Feral cat rehabilitators have techniques that will turn a feral cat into a house cat in mere weeks, and now there are books about how to achieve this (with patience and a few simple tricks). So if cats can do it, perhaps rabbits can as well. Of course, Hohepa was never a feral rabbit and certainly not a wild rabbit, but he *was* indifferent to us and the other animals living with him. I still sometimes worry that he is not living the best possible life for a rabbit. But when a friend dropped by and watched Hohepa hop from the beach to our garden to the inside of our house and then into Ilan's lap for a cuddle, she said, "That's one lucky bunny!" I think she was probably right. Rabbits don't often get to be indoor/outdoor rabbits roaming an entire beach with friends, do they?

A few days later, our little menagerie was going for a stroll along the beach when Mika's best friend, Bella the neighbor dog, came racing along, heading not for Mika but for Hohepa. Hohepa froze, and Bella seemed poised to make a fatal pounce. I was too far ahead to get back in time to stop it, but Mika took off like a shot. She placed herself between Hohepa and Bella and growled at her erstwhile friend. "Touch her and you're dead," was the look she gave. Bella backed off. Wow! Mika protected the rabbit! It was unexpected and actually quite touching. I wanted to (I did) kiss Mika for her kindness. What other rabbit has a guard-dog friend?

———

UNLIKE HOHEPA, Mika had always been interested in us and the animals surrounding her, even as a puppy. She matured and improved, but she underwent no major transformation of personality, no change of soul, as Hohepa and the cats seemed to. She was a dog, after all, an animal predestined by evolution to extreme sociability. I would like to believe that it was our peaceful environment that encouraged her to become so eager to please all other dogs she met (except when she was called on to protect one of her friends). She would positively grovel at their feet, licking their faces, placating them should she so much as bump against them by mistake, and begging them to like her and see her as no threat. I liked this behavior. I was proud of it. But that was not why Mika did it. She did it because this was the character she had "inherited." No doubt we reinforced it. We rewarded it. We approved, and she knew that. I am sure we could have turned her into an aggressive and unpleasant dog. But we did not really alter her character. She grew up with all the other animals in our house and was prepared now to meet them on friendly terms. Her environment did not change her, but it enriched her.

Mika's behavior around humans, on the other hand, left much to be desired. She would often bark aggressively, and for no discernible reason, at people walking along the beach. If she was not tied up, she would sometimes rush up to them with less than friendly intent. I would always say, "Don't worry, she's very friendly," because I was so used to saying this about other dogs we had lived with, but in Mika's case I was not so sure. I wondered if she had had an unhappy childhood before she came to live with us. I didn't want to believe she was aggressive toward humans because of her own nature. She was still just a puppy, I told myself, hoping I was not indulging in a delusion.

I would have liked to understand the idea of Mika's "nature" better, but it posed many puzzles. When she seemed mild, we liked to believe it was because of the "upbringing" we gave her. When she turned nasty, we started to wonder about her inherited character. Friends who knew her would say things like "Look at her jaw. She has some pit bull in her. No wonder she is aggressive." But if they were right, wouldn't this mean she would have been aggressive toward other animals, too? Leila, a great believer in early childhood experiences as a shaper of character, thought Mika's earliest days were responsible for who she had become. Other friends, who swore by training, insisted that we had not asserted dominance early enough. Robyn Haworth had a more sophisticated version of this argument.

She said that by not teaching Mika her place in our "pack," we confused her, and she believed it was her duty to protect us, since we could not do this for ourselves. She had taken over the leadership of our family, given our failure to do so. The truth was that Mika was far more docile and better behaved around both Robyn and Conny, a dog trainer with beliefs similar to Robyn's. Was it also not possible that Mika simply came into the world with a certain character, or at least certain tendencies, that we had failed to curtail or perhaps even unknowingly encouraged? I was not sure. But the purpose of this experiment was not to see if a dog could be well behaved with humans (we know that dogs can be), but rather if a dog could learn tolerance toward natural enemies in the animal world. In that we had succeeded. This will come as no surprise to dog people.

I WAS NOT CERTAIN about Kia the rat. Experience had taught her that Megala was her mortal enemy, and she made that evident every time she saw him. She would shake and race away into some corner of my clothes when she even smelled him. But she showed no such fear of either Tamaiti or Moko. She often went nose to nose with Moko, as if trying to figure out what kind of cat he was. She was wary, but not really scared. Moko was curious, too, and clearly not a threat. Kia would even seem prepared to play, as she reached up to put her small paws on Mika's large nose. Mika was not sure what to make of this. It was not the usual call to play that she recognized. Perhaps one day she would, though, and they would go racing together across the beach.

News bulletin: Less than two weeks after I wrote the previous paragraph, Kia became the second of our animals to be transformed. She must have decided to force the situation with Mika, something I suspected had been brewing in her mind for some time. I was holding Kia in the TV room when she suddenly leapt off my lap and ran over to Mika, who was asleep on a pillow in the corner. She rushed around to his nose and began batting it playfully. Before, she would touch it tentatively, but now she was making it clear that she had a game in mind. Mika woke up, saw what was taking place, and began to wag her tail furiously, as if to say, "I wondered when you would come around." They then began a series of games, where Mika would chase Kia, and then Kia would chase Mika. Such a strange sight, this tiny rat and the large frisky dog, playing. She now took enormous pleasure in climbing on Mika's feet and reaching up to her, as if asking her to pick her up. (See page 134 for a picture of one of their meetings.) She had a sense of humor. Imagine, a rat with a sense of humor! But I know that people who live with and love rats would not be the least surprised.

As for Tamaiti, he was always easygoing and happy to be friends with all the other animals, even the rat. He simply found the room for his personality to develop to its full limits. I am sure he would have been the same cat no matter where he had been brought up. Of course, he would probably not have tolerated rats, but he was so pleasant a character that I am sure

it would not have taken much to teach him tolerance under any circumstances, with his live-and-let-live personality. He was also vastly entertaining on walks. He would lag behind on purpose, then come thundering past us, his paws making a good imitation of a herd of buffalo. He would stop, look for the nearest tree, then rush to it, leap into the branches, and climb the trunk right to the top, then come down at breakneck speed. Then he would saunter over and wait for the ever forthcoming praise.

Then there came a night when for the first time Kia and Tamaiti positively reveled in each other. We were watching a video, with Kia ensconced in the hood of my jogging suit, when Tamaiti walked slowly into the room, looking for a companion to play with. He gave his playful little meow, pranced about, rolled on his back, leapt into the air, raced from couch cushion to couch cushion. To our surprise, Kia jumped out of the hood and ran up to Tamaiti, who was taken aback at first, but then suddenly rolled over and lifted Kia gently into the air with his paws. Kia jumped down, circled the room like a kid with a new bike, then rushed over to Tamaiti and tried to climb up his nose. Mika followed the action with utter fascination, waiting for her turn to play with Kia. They played like this for fifteen minutes. All of us who saw it were astonished. Our friend and neighbor Conny (with Baxter the poodle) was there and remarked that if we had had a video of the whole sequence, we would be millionaires, it was so unusual. Kia now positively glows with the friendship. She looks about with calm confidence, whereas before she was much more furtive, always ready to flee. This has been yet another boon, one completely unforeseen.

Tamaiti was a big cat now that she was fully grown and most impressive to look at, with her very large, bright blue eyes. She would walk regally into a room and expect to be noticed. She was. She had no faults that I could discover, not even vanity, so I don't believe she demanded your attention, she just got it naturally and kept it without artifice. She was a most unusual cat. I have heard somebody complain that she was lacking in personality, and I had to think about this for a minute. I suppose there was some truth to the comment. A strong personality usually implies some sort of conflict, and Tamaiti did not cause or incite conflict. You could say she was placid, but another word equally apposite would be "calm." Where there was Tamaiti, there was no strife. Was a lack of strife boring? Well, I suppose to some people it was. You might claim that all happy cats were alike and only the unhappy ones were interesting. Tamaiti was a happy cat. It was true there was no edge to her, the way there was to both Moko and Megala. If you made a wrong move in their presence, they were likely to punish you, physically but also emotionally. They would snub you, walk away from you. Such a thing would never have occurred to Tamaiti.

Again, I had to ask, was Tamaiti so gentle, friendly, and of such a sweet disposition because of breeding, because she was born that way, or because of the way she had been brought up? I suppose it is the same question we ask about our own children and the children of other people. In fact, we can ask it of our dogs and of all our friends. Of every living creature, in fact. Politically, I was inclined to believe in nurture. Now that I have children, however, I am forced to give more credence to nature. And having lived with so many different dogs and cats, I have to wonder about breeding as well. It is all rather confusing, and nothing I have ever read has convinced me one way or the other. In any event, what I know for certain is that whether or not our children or our animals come into the world with their personalities already formed does not absolve us from giving them the best possible life, whether it makes an obvious difference or not. That is our moral duty regardless of how the question of nature vs. nurture is answered (if it ever is).

I have often wondered whether some animals are better than some humans when it comes to certain major emotions. Contentment always seemed to me to be one of those emotions that cats manage better than humans. It is not just that cats *seem* more relaxed and content than most humans; they actually *are*. A little bit of emulation is in order here. But it is not only cats. All animals are good at contentment, and that is probably because it does not take that much to make them content. Being surrounded by friends after a copious meal in a safe setting will do it. Come to think of it, that would pretty much do the trick for humans as well. The difference is that humans are aware of their contentment, or can be made aware of it. It is a question of considerable philosophical interest whether the same is true of animals in general. Are they "aware" (in the full sense of that word) of their happiness? Do they reflect upon it and compare it with other times when they were not content, or not as content as they are at the time of asking the question? That much is pretty unlikely. But does it matter? What are the advantages of human awareness in the full sense of the word? It is probable that animals know when they are *un*happy or *not* content, then strive to alter that situation, just as humans do, and are probably just as successful at it as humans without benefit of awareness in general.

Kia now seemed possessed with the desire to play. As I have said, she was terrified of Megala. But when she was in her cage and Megala came next to it, she would extend her tiny fingernail through the cage and entice Megala over. She then would throw herself against the bars of her cage as if she wanted to get at Megala. It was a game, and Megala played back. If Megala went to the other side of the cage, Kia would rush over to continue her pretend assaults. Could I be sure? Could she have been attempting to fight with Megala? That was not impossible, I suppose, but she seemed so unstressed that I was sure she was playing.

The most radical change of all, however, was to be found in my wife, Leila. She went from finding the idea of a rat slightly gross to wanting Kia with her at just about all times, especially at night. Here was a German pediatrician not objecting to having a bit of rat pee and poop in her bed at night. That was pretty amazing! I wish I could say that she underwent a similar change of heart about all the other animals, but she did not. She resisted Mika's charms and was not a great fan of the chickens, especially when they roosted and soiled her favorite Indian spread on the living room couch. She would shoo them out of the house while they made indignant noises, making us all conscious of their offended dignity. Hohepa she liked to see exclusively outside, and the cats were now tolerable to her only because they no longer hunted. A deeply committed vegetarian, Leila was the person most intolerant of carnivores in our family. Tamaiti, of course, was an exception. Nobody could remain indifferent to Tamaiti. Besides, while he ate cat food, he never hunted and never hurt any other animal. He would even release flies after he caught them!

Because of Manu's early exposure to Tamaiti, Mika, Hohepa, Ora and Kia, and Moa and Moana, he would, I was sure, love animals throughout his life. The same, I hoped, would be true for Ilan, though I could not be sure, since this exposure came later for him. As for me, well, I had some prejudices confirmed, certain biases strengthened, but most important, I believe I learned an important message from our little menagerie: Exposure, familiarity, knowledge, and education in the form of direct experience may hold the secret to peaceable coexistence —for humans as well.

How differently do humans learn from the ways animals learn? For a long time, we thought there was no such thing as animal culture—that is, traditions handed down from one animal to another via methods we only dimly understood. Now we know that it happens, certainly among primates, but probably among most other animals as well. In fact, even fish have cultural transmission, as revealed through the work of Culum Brown from the University of Edinburgh: Coral reef fish, for example, have migration paths "between feeding and resting sites that have been shown to be culturally transmitted" (see *NewScientist,* June 12, 2004). Was this so different from socialization in human terms?

Some friends, when they learned that Ilan and Manu were vegetarian, accused me of "brainwashing" them. I thought about this and wondered if they were right. But then I realized that an appropriate response could be: As opposed to what? If we served them meat, wouldn't we be socializing them to be carnivores? Of course, the goal was for Ilan and Manu to make their own choices. But until they were able to do so, what *we* chose for them would continue to have a strong influence now and perhaps later on what *they* chose for themselves. This was true for what they read, how they played, what they wore—in short, just about everything that happened to them until they left home was a form of acculturation or socialization. Every parent makes these choices. Call it brainwashing if you will, but no society has ever managed otherwise or figured out a different way.

I am not sure how different the process of acculturation is for animals. Perhaps less than we think. They learn what to eat and what to avoid from their parents. They learn where to live from their society. They even adopt the prejudices of their parents and their early companions in much the same way human children do. Perhaps the major difference is that some animals seem to develop a rigid behavioral pattern early in life (as do some humans), whereas, ideally, humans remain capable of major change, both in behavior and in attitude, into old age.

Prejudices die, even among animals, when direct experience shows them something that their tradition (or their instincts) tells them is not so. That is the amazing thing. Of course, humans are animals, and yes, we are as prone to an "us/them" mentality as any other animal. There is an in-group and an out-group, kin and nonkin. Whether we are acculturated into this knowledge, as is undoubtedly the case with humans, or born with it, as is undoubtedly the case with animals, what I have learned—the most important lesson of all—

is that it is not immutable. We, animals and humans, can change. I have seen it with my own eyes in this "little experiment with the big ideas."

My goal was to learn something about the roots of tolerance, friendship, and even compassion in humans from this project of raising animals together. The great neurophysiologist Jaak Panksepp writes: "As every young child knows, play is the very source of joy, and there should be little doubt that rats feel such positive emotions, as do all mammals. . . . They seek out what makes them feel good, and they avoid what makes them feel bad. This may seem to be a simple and self-evident fact, but it's also a profound truth of nature." He laments that so many scientists who use animals in their research refuse to acknowledge this. Do the animals know they are feeling pleasure? Well, of course. As Panksepp notes,* evolution built emotions into the nervous system at the very foundation of that mysterious process we call consciousness. I think by "at" he means "as," and I interpret this to mean: No emotions, no consciousness. I have brought joy to the animals sharing my home, and they have brought joy to one another and to me.

YESTERDAY, Thursday, June 8, 2004, the rest of the family went off on a visit and I was on my own with the animals. It was the middle of winter, but the weather was mild and sunny, the temperature a lovely sixty-eight degrees. It was late afternoon,

*In *The Smile of a Dolphin: Remarkable Accounts of Animal Emotions.* Edited by Marc Bekoff, foreword by Stephen Jay Gould. N.Y.: Discovery Books, 2000, p. 147.

and the sun was streaming into the living room. It was completely still. The ocean in front of our house was flat and calm. Everything was quiet. I was sitting on the sofa, reading. I was wearing my jogging sweatshirt, with a hood. Inside was snuggled Kia the rat. Tamaiti and Hohepa were curled up together on the sofa next to me. Next to them was Mika, fast asleep. Moko and Megala were lying together on the other sofa, dozing. Moa and Moana the chickens were lying still on the rug at my feet. There was a soft knock on the front door, and a visitor who had never been to the house before opened the door and walked in. Everybody looked up. She gasped as if she had seen a ghost.

"What is this," she asked, "the peaceable kingdom?"

Exactly.

FIVE

All Good Things
Must End

THERE HAS BEEN yet another disturbing new development in the rules about dogs in the city of Auckland, of which our beach is a part. The bad news is that owners (their word, not mine) who allow their dogs off leash in any but a designated area will incur not only a hefty fine of US$300 but, if they are on the beach, another US$300 on top of the first fine. This is depressing for many reasons, not the least being that Mika is used to being off leash all day. Perhaps this is not a good thing, but we have wanted Mika to have as much freedom as possible, the same goal we have sought for all the animals who live with us. The good news is that our beach, Karaka Bay Beach, is to be designated a leash-free area. Since there are few such areas, people with dogs will flock to our beach. That is good for Mika, but it is very bad news for the rabbit and the chickens.

Throughout this project, I had been fighting two contrary

impulses, one to "conduct the experiment," as it were, as cleanly as possible, and the second to give the animals the best life they could possibly have. The two, I am beginning to understand, have not always been compatible. When our family was in the north of the North Island of New Zealand, in the Hokianga, we stayed at a backpacker's hostel called the Tree House, run by a wonderful Australian scholar of birds, Phil Evans. He had many kinds of birds running loose on his magnificent property—guinea fowl, chickens, ducks, doves, and others on acres and acres of woods, streams, ponds, and rain forest. It was a true paradise.

Later, Phil came for a visit and saw our little peaceable kingdom, including Hohepa and the chooks. After studying the situation, he said gently, "Don't you think Hohepa the rabbit and the two chooks would be better off at my place, free of any danger that they inevitably meet on a public beach in Auckland, especially one that is about to see a huge influx of dogs?"

It was one of those dazzling questions, not meant to hurt, but I saw immediately that he was right. So in July, when our family was scheduled to leave for Europe, where Leila's family awaited us, Phil was going to take Hohepa and the chickens to his extraordinary slice of paradise. I had and would fully utilize visitation rights. But I could not argue against him, even though Hohepa was one very fast rabbit. He had been chased by dogs before, and he had an amazing zigzag technique that allowed him to escape. So far. But sooner or later Hohepa would have been bound to come to an untimely death, with all the new dogs who would be coming down to the beach, unaware of his special status as Rabbit of Karaka Bay. Hohepa was used to doing whatever he wanted, wandering wherever he liked. He would be hunted, no doubt about it, and sooner or later he would meet his match, and none of us would have been able to bear the consequences. He would lose his best friend, Tamaiti, but was friendship worth more than life? And now that he was a fully socialized rabbit, we were certain he would make new friends quickly.

The chickens were even more vulnerable. Moa would strut about as if he owned the beach, and most of the regular inhabitants here respected his rights. But it would not take much for a large dog to end Moa's glory days. Moana would have pined away, I was certain. She could not have lived without her constant companion.

The logic was irresistible. Still, it was sad for our family. We had become so attached. How about the animals themselves? Would they feel the same way? I didn't know, but I was sure it would be difficult for Hohepa and Tamaiti. I suspected that once Hohepa and the chickens saw their new home (a five-hour drive from Auckland), they would forget us in a second. But we would not forget them and how they had enriched our lives.

It had now been two months, and I had had several updates from Phil. Moa and Moana had been reclusive for a while, preferring their own company and not mixing with the other birds. But after about a month that changed, and they had become happily part of a much larger flock. They would wander about the property all day and bring themselves into a protective shed only for the night. No neighbors complained about the crowing, either.

Hohepa was not able to move to his new home until almost a month after the chickens were already there. We had wanted him to be neutered first, because there were wild rabbits on Phil's property and we did not want him contributing to the population. The university vet assured us that after neutering, Hohepa would be an even more docile rabbit and would stop peeing in the house (though I don't think Phil planned to have him come into his house much). Tony Watkins, our architect neighbor, drove him to Phil's. When Hohepa was let out of the car, he sniffed around for a few minutes, unfazed by his new surroundings, and then suddenly, Moa and Moana, who had been in a far corner of the property, came racing up and greeted him much as we would greet a long-lost friend. Phil and Tony reported that they all seemed mighty pleased to see one another.

Ilan sobbed when he learned that Hohepa and the chickens had to go, but we explained that it was their happiness, not ours, that counted for more. With safety added to the equation, it seemed obvious that we had little choice. When Ilan heard the latest, that Moa and Moana now have four baby chicks, he was thrilled. They are looking after the chicks together! Moa is a very protective father and will not allow anybody, human or animal, to come too close to the babies.

Hohepa has now done more than settle in. He is the king!

He sits all day on the deck and rushes up to every new guest who arrives at the hostel. They always assume he is a small dog coming to greet them, until they see the large ears and realize he is a bunny, the most friendly bunny they have ever seen. He spends his days on the deck receiving homage from all his new friends, and then at night he takes off into the forest to forage. Come morning, he is always back. Phil does not know how he ever managed without Hohepa, and I feel nothing but paternal pride.

But now comes the most difficult part of this book for me to write. I have had to come to terms with what two of the people most intimately involved in the project, my friends Conny and Robyn, have said about Mika. Both are dog people, and both have noticed that Mika is not doing well here. By that they mean that she does not seem as happy as she could be. When they first brought it up, I was hurt. But as soon as they explained, I realized they were right. When Mika is with either of them, her tail never stops wagging. She is quick to obey, eager to play, willing to learn—in short, she is the working dog she was clearly meant to be. With us, both claimed (as I mentioned before) that there was confusion. Is that true? Yes, of course. I am not a great believer in discipline, or perhaps it is merely that I do not have the temperament for giving orders, for expecting to be obeyed, for hierarchy and its various manifestations. But dogs are hierarchical, Conny and Robyn insisted, and they are right. Dogs recognize leadership and insist upon it. They positively expect it; they thrive on it. They are confused without it.

And I was not providing it. Nor was any other member of my family.

Conny and Robyn's hypothesis was that Mika felt unprotected. In this state, she felt that she had to be the boss and to protect herself as well as us from all strangers; hence her ceaseless barking at anybody who passed our house or was simply walking along the beach. No matter how often I told her not to, she continued to bark. In the presence of either Conny or Robyn she would not do this, or at least she would desist the minute they told her to. In other words, she recognized their authority and submitted to it. It was just a hypothesis, but in the absence of anything that made better sense, I had to agree with them. The upshot is that we all felt Mika would be happier with Conny or Robyn. In fact, even as I write, Mika is living temporarily at Robyn's house, with Mika's friend Missy. They are in heaven together, as I have seen on my visits. Robyn wants to try it out for a few months, and if it is too much for her with her doves, her cats, her rabbit, her dog, and her three children, not to mention an unbelievably busy schedule, then Conny will take over in November. (November has come and gone, and Robyn cannot bear parting with Mika. It looks as if she is there to stay; but Conny will take her for a special "search and rescue" course for dogs. She thinks she has a special aptitude for this.)

Conny says she is in love with Mika, and that is the only reason to have a dog. I have to agree. As much as I wanted to be, I am not in love with her, nor is any member of our family. That is the downside of our plugging for egalitarianism in our house. Mika "acts out," as therapists like to say of patients who do difficult and dangerous things outside the therapy hour. She snaps at children; she growls at two-year-old Manu; she threatens everyone who comes to the door; she even chases our neighbors up the path as they leave their houses. In short, she behaves abominably. And who is to blame? *We* are, clearly.

Why did this not happen with the three dogs I wrote about in *Dogs Never Lie About Love*? Because with them I spent my entire day. I was theirs. I took them everywhere, walked all day long with them. It was my job for two years, and I took it seriously. It is not so much that I was their leader, but I was definitely a senior member of the pack. Mika, they think, does not know her place in our house but instantly recognizes it in the other two households.

I will continue to be a part of Mika's life, just not the main part. There is something sad about this, some sense on my part and on Leila's part that we have failed somehow. I think failure is not too strong a word for what has happened here. Funny, I always thought of myself as a dog person, but I actually do better with cats. Our three cats are so independent that we can all lead separate lives and come together only when it is mutually desired. That is very satisfactory for me. I love sleeping with the cats. I love when they come for walks along the beach with me. But I also love not having to worry every minute what they will do with themselves should I leave them alone. That was my constant preoccupation with Mika. What will Mika do for the next hour while I work on my book? How can we leave Mika at home to go to a movie? Can I go shopping and leave Mika here? I was in a constant state of guilt. This was not good for Mika, and it was not making me or the family happy, either.

This experiment, however, was not meant for my pleasure. While I do get pleasure from the companionship of animals, in this case I was trying to determine how animals from different species learn to tolerate one another. It was not a purely scientific experiment, but neither was it idle speculation or simply an excuse to spend a year with fun animals. I set out to determine whether tolerance was possible among "natural enemies."

So what had I learned about tolerance, play, friendship, and becoming soul mates? I made a list. First, the eight rules of tolerance:

1. Stay out of the way.
2. Don't pick a fight.
3. If challenged, walk away.
4. Avoid eye contact.
5. If your enemy is diurnal, learn to be nocturnal.
6. Vice versa.
7. Possess nothing the other wants.
8. Draw the line at hurting kids: I will fight to the death.

After tolerance is achieved comes play. Here are the nine rules of play:

1. Know when to quit.
2. Learn how to handicap.
3. Learn what frightens the other (cat claws).
4. Don't let it get to you. It's just a game; you mustn't take it seriously (cats have trouble with this one—escalation is always a risk in cat games).
5. Don't eat your playmate.
6. Pay attention to the signals on the other side—for instance, "enough" and "quit."
7. Don't suddenly change the rules.
8. Don't be a sore loser.
9. Remember: It's only a game.

And if play succeeds, we can move on to the eight rules of friendship:

1. Learn the rules of your opposite number.
2. Recognize that danger is no longer relevant.
3. Take your time.
4. One step at a time.
5. Apologize often by learning the other's words, gestures, sounds, or postures for "I'm sorry."
6. Acknowledge mistakes.
7. Make the offer of friendship more than once.
8. Express curiosity about what the other is like.

As for the ten rules of becoming soul mates, or best friends, well, there are none. It either happens (rarely) or it doesn't (fre-

quently). If it does happen, consider it a miracle you have been privileged to observe.

Speaking of miracles, Megala, the one cat who had refused to join our peaceable kingdom, has recently provided us with one. We were at our country house, where Kia the rat has a little wooden structure, almost like a tiny cave, on the kitchen counter, and where she likes to drag various bits of food and drink her soy milk. Yesterday was a spectacular day, and we were all outside on the deck overlooking our swimming pond. Kia, who spends most of her time with us, at this moment happened to be in her cave back in the kitchen. I looked through the kitchen window from the deck and was shocked to see Megala sitting up on the counter. We ran into the house, but were stopped cold by a wonderful sight: Kia came out of her cave, raised up on her hind legs, and tentatively started sniffing

Megala's nose. Megala did what leopards do when they want to make friends: He butted her tiny face, rolled over, and started to purr. Kia approached closer, and gave him a small lick. The deal was sealed: friends for life! This was a transformation I would not have thought possible. I guess Megala finally decided there was nothing like friendship across the species barrier, and who could possibly disagree?

Epilogue:
Applying the Results
to Humans

One of my original reasons for undertaking this "experiment" was to show by example of seven young animals born "natural enemies" that humans from different cultures, ethnic groups, nationalities, religions, and races might also be able to live together as friends if they were socialized into this view. Does this, in fact, bear out?

No one understands the origins of human conflict, nor is there any obvious solution in sight. So of course I am not claiming to have solved the problem or discerned a cure, but the comparisons with animals may yet prove helpful or lead to further insight. After all, we are alike in many ways, so why could we not learn from this one major difference, from this advantage that animals have over humans? For too long, scientists have said things like "Humans are the only animal to have speech, the only animal to have tools, the only animal to transmit culture." All of these claims have been quietly abandoned in the last twenty years or so. A claim that one doesn't often see made, however, is "Humans are the only animal to engage in wars, genocide, torture, and crimes against humanity." Yet here is a claim that is *not* likely to dissolve as we learn more about animals. The question can legitimately be asked why it has hardly been mentioned. Perhaps it is because even asking the question is an affront to human vanity. Genocide is not a distinction we covet for ourselves to differentiate us from the beasts. The adjective *beastly* has rarely been used with any degree of accuracy or even any sense at all, but it misses the mark when applied to human genocide and human torture. "They behaved like animals" is a senseless comment one frequently encounters when humans behave badly toward one another.

I am aware that my readers do not need a reminder of the horrors of the twentieth century. Nevertheless, to better understand the comparisons and contrasts with animal societies, it might be useful to devote a short paragraph to each of the major atrocities to remind ourselves of the simple facts of what the famous Marxist historian Eric Hobsbawm has called "the most extraordinary and terrible century in human history."* And since I have invoked the name of this scholar of the twentieth century, let me borrow from him and add to one of his

---

* *Interesting Times: A Twentieth-Century Life* by Eric Hobsbawm (considered a leading twentieth-century historian, but one who evidently shied away from including in his writings the crimes of Stalin). N.Y.: Pantheon, 2003, p. 11.

central insights that clarifies greatly the distinction between humans and animals. Hobsbawm noted that "emancipated and assimilated Viennese Jews talked about Eastern Jews as of some other species." *Some other species.* There, in three words, is the explanation and also the most terrible indictment of human behavior in the last century. My addition is this: In making humans a different species—namely, an animal species—the Nazi perpetrators were justifying their cruelty, their murder, their tyranny, on the grounds that the people targeted for extinction or destruction were *animals.* Underlying this claim is the assumption that humans are always and everywhere entitled to eliminate any animal species they choose.

I am speaking here not of the casualties of wars, but of the deliberate killing of innocent civilians *by their own or another legitimate government for reasons that were entirely fantasy-driven.* Consider the bare figures: In the twentieth century, 61,911,000* people were murdered by the Soviet Union, 38,702,000 by the Chinese Communists, 10,214,000 by the Chinese Nationalists, 17,000,000 by the German Nazis, and 5,890,000 by the Japanese militarists. This is hardly a complete reckoning, but already the figure is more than 100,000,000 people who have been murdered, usually by their own government, since 1900. Let us look at some of the "outstanding" events of the twentieth century.

---

*See *Humanity: A Moral History of the Twentieth Century* by Jonathan Glover. London: Jonathan Cape, 1999, p. 237.

1. 1915: Of a total population of 2.5 million, 1.5 million Armenians were murdered by the "Young Turk" government in the final years (1915–1917) of the Ottoman Empire. Hitler's famous 1939 quote "Who today remembers the Armenians?" could be answered: the Armenians. (What he actually said was reported by *The New York Times* on November 24, 1945: "I have sent to the East my 'Death Head Units' with the order to kill without pity or mercy all men, women, and children of the Polish race or language. Only in such a way will we win the vital space we need. Who still talks nowadays of the extermination of the Armenians?"

2. 1933–1945: Before the Nazis killed six million Jews, they first murdered nearly three hundred thousand German citizens who were deemed "mentally ill" or "deformed" or "defective" and whom psychiatrists and other doctors considered to have "lives not worth living"—one of the most evil and destructive phrases of our time.

3. The 1930s: While it defies belief, objective estimates indicate that the Soviet Union killed 9.5 million "enemies of the people" in this decade, many of whom "confessed" to their "crimes" in an orgy of psychological flagellation that has still not been explained or perhaps even completely understood.

4. 1975: Approximately 1.7 million Cambodians, almost 20 percent of the population, were massacred when Pol Pot (Brother Number One) and the Khmer Rouge, his army of

peasant teenagers, marched into Phnom Penh on April 17, 1975.

Our attempts to understand these murderous outbreaks, to explain why they happened, seem doomed to fail. Was the Turkish murder of the Armenians politically motivated? No, for politically uninvolved women and children were murdered as well. Why did Hitler hate the Jews so? In spite of more than a hundred thousand books written about the Holocaust, we don't know. How could Stalin have convinced people he was about to execute—not every time, to be sure, but often enough—to confess to crimes they never committed? Why did he want them dead, and why were so many people willing to act in his name and countless others, including leading intellectuals, to condone, rationalize, or cast their eyes away from what he did?

How many people did Robert Mugabe, still the president of Zimbabwe, kill in Matabeleland (people whose main sins seem to have been that they voted consistently against his ruling party, ZANU-PF)? A hundred thousand, at least. He was Shona speaking, and he and his ethnic exterminators, the red bereted Fifth Brigade, were Ndebele speaking. How do we account for the murders? Was it political hatred, linguistic hatred, or something entirely different that eludes classification?

Did the Serbs really murder Kosovars because King Lazar lost the Battle of Kosovo to the invading Turks *six centuries ago?* To any outsider, the people of ex-Yugoslavia seemed remarkably similar: The language appeared identical (are not Serbian and Croatian just dialects of the same language?), they came from similar stock, they had similar religions. To make the other "other," we have been told, is at the root of all hatred. But were these people "other"? Is this an example of what Freud called *le narcissisme des petites différences?**

Do we understand today what caused the massacres by the Hutu of the Tutsi in Rwanda? Eight hundred thousand Tutsis of both sexes and all ages were slaughtered by the Hutu in a ninety-day rampage in the spring of 1994. Former Rwandan prime minister Jean Kambanda was the first person in history to plead guilty to the charge of genocide. He knew no more than his jurors why he did what he did and why it was so easy to find accomplices.

Dr. Mohammed Mahathir of Malaysia is interested only in what he calls *bramaputras,* the "sons of the soil," and not alien species such as Asians and Chinese Malaysians, who are not *real* Malays. Needless to say, he detests Jews, homosexuals, and Europeans as well. The thesis of the "other" is seen here again in stark form.

The Ethiopian colonel Mengistu Haile Mariam, today living in exile in Zimbabwe, began a campaign of terror when he overthrew Haile Selassie in 1974. Human Rights Watch estimated that he and his Dergue ("Committee") killed at least half a million civilian "reactionaries" and other enemies of the

---

*For Bosnia, see Roy Gutman's prize-winning series of articles in *Newsday,* collected in book form as *A Witness to Genocide.* N.Y.: Macmillan, 1993.

people between 1976 and 1991, when he was deposed. Other, enemies, foreign, not like us, evil—it almost seems as if we as a species have been given language to invent excuses for hatred.

In my travels through Europe, I have always been surprised at how much dislike there seemed to be for other citizens of the *same* country for some perceived fault, usually the mistake of having been born in a different part of the country. In Belgium, the Flemish and the French seemed to hate each other with glee. Southern Germans disliked northern Germans. In France, those from the Midi spoke contemptuously of the Parisians. Even in Italy, when I told a cabdriver in Milano that he was the friendliest person I had yet met in that northern town, he told me proudly, "*Ma, signore, io sono meridionale!*" ("But, sir, I am from the south!"), and then went on to heap abuse on the northern Italians.

Many buildings in the American South still fly the Confederate flag, symbol of a racist past, with considerable pride and not a little hatred of the North, still palpable 140 years after the end of the Civil War.

The Canadian judge Rosalie Abella told a conference on genocide: "All over the world, in the name of religion, domestic sovereignty, national interest, economic exigency or sheer arrogance, men, women and children are being slaughtered, abused, imprisoned, terrorized, and exploited. With impunity."*

---

*Quoted in *Long Shadows: Truth, Lies, and History* by Erna Paris. London: Bloomsbury, 2000.

I am hardly the first to notice that such atrocities are foreign to any known animal species. But it strikes people, even
people with no particular interest in animal behavior, with
great force when they first notice it. When the South African
writer Christopher Hope, writing about these and other atrocities in *Brother Under the Skin: Travels in Tyranny,* was visiting
Victoria Falls in Zimbabwe in 2002, he was warned about the
wild elephants wandering along the roads. He remarked: "I
wasn't particularly worried. Generally, they are shy and benign
creatures, they do not mount roadblocks, or drop the bodies of
their victims down mine-shafts, or promise them heaven and
send them home hungry."

Similar comments about the lack of murderous intent, the
absence of genocide, among animals are nearly a cliché. Yet it is
true and deserves to be rescued from appearing to be merely a
cliché, for in reality it is more than that. Animals prey upon
one another, of course. The predator/prey relationship is essential to many (not all) animal societies. But the reason is clear:
food. There is nothing beyond that. There is no attempt to
demonize the preyed upon. No education of young lions in the
evil ways of impalas. There are no schools of torture for kittens
to learn to dismember rats. The eagle is not convinced of his
superior abilities before he makes his devastating dive. And
when the brief mayhem is over, calm returns to the forest or
jungle or field. The animals will not fraternize, perhaps, but
neither will they glare. Indifference except by necessity seems
to be the motto of most animals. The animals know the other

species, they are familiar with them and appear to have no need to see them as other than they are. They are not curious, but neither do they hold distorted views. They have achieved a kind of equanimity. What happened to the human species?

"Familiarity?" a cynic will perhaps throw at me, mocking my suggestion that these people who so hate one another were not familiar with one another, that all they needed was exposure at the right time and they would be cured of their bloodlust, their narrow-mindedness, their murderous hatreds, their xenophobias, and their tribal insularity. Do I really believe that? I, a former psychoanalyst, chronicler of human weakness among psychologists? Or am I merely a sentimentalist, determined at any price, even wild distortion, to show the superior wisdom and behavior of our animal cousins?

My critics may have a point. I read, but reluctantly, about the murderous raids of baboons and chimpanzees; about rape by mallard ducks; about infanticide among the lions. I know these things exist, but I hesitate to accord them the same paradigmatic significance that rape, murder, and child abuse have been accorded in human societies. It is possible I am hiding my head in the sands of ignorance, but from my reading in this disquieting field, I also believe the numbers are still small. Yes, some male lions kill the young of strange females, to force them into estrus and thus produce their own progeny. But the number of male lions who do this is still smaller than the number who do not. Most species of fowl do *not* have any form of forced intercourse. And *most* primates do not assault with murderous intent other primates. Above all, it is the systematic nature of the human tragedies that cries out for explanation and for a contrasting comparison with animals. Perhaps animals have solved a problem we have not. What could be wrong with that? Is it not worth a thought, at least? And if the Darwinian explanation of evolved selfishness and evolved hatreds and evolved lack of compassion does *not* apply to animals, perhaps the same is true of humans.

Can it be that all such human hatred is merely the product of evolution? There is an old Arab saying: "Me and my cousin against the stranger; me and my brother against my cousin." No doubt there are evolutionary roots to some human hatreds, but it is difficult to explain how or why they turn so quickly to internecine fraternal hatred. It does not take long for brother to turn against brother.

When the first Crusaders took Jerusalem in 1099, they massacred all the Jews and Muslims in the city, men, women, and children, a good example of "me and my cousin against the stranger": "The Crusaders . . . rushed through the streets and into the houses and mosques killing all that they met, men, women, and children alike. All that afternoon and all through the night the massacre continued. Tancred's banner was no protection to the refugees in the mosque of al-Aqsa. Early next morning a band of Crusaders forced an entry into the mosque and slew everyone. . . . The Jews of Jerusalem fled in a body to their chief synagogue. But they were held to have aided the Moslems; and no mercy was shown to them. The building was set on fire and they were all burnt within. The massacre at Jerusalem profoundly impressed the entire world. No one can say how many victims it involved; but it emptied Jerusalem of its Moslem and Jewish inhabitants."*

Now it was time to turn against the cousin: As soon as victory was secure, the Latin Church and the Eastern Church began fighting among themselves! As the sociobiologists (now called evolutionary biologists) put it, group-living animals, either for self-survival or in their own "genetic self-interest," will cooperate only within their group, not outside of it.† Rape, slavery, and even fighting wars are all "natural" behaviors in the sense that human beings have been engaging in them for all of recorded history and in prehistory as well. Yes, it is part of our biological inheritance. But that doesn't mean it is wrong (even if we can say it is contrary to nature) to renounce them. "Natural" does not necessarily translate into "desirable." Even if the word *natural* is used with scientific precision and accuracy, it is still primarily a historical adjective (or concept), not an ethical one.

Does any animal know it belongs to a specific species? Of course. But animals do not know this the way a Frenchman

---

*A History of the Crusades: Volume I: The First Crusade and the Foundation of the Kingdom of Jerusalem by Steven Runciman. Cambridge: Cambridge University Press, 1951, p. 287 *ff.* Brilliant as this three-volume work of historical scholarship is, I find it depressing that Runciman never sums up, never tells us what his unparalleled knowledge has led him to understand about the folly of human beings. He must have thought about it but does not give us the benefit of his wisdom.

†The title of an edited volume says it all: *The Sociobiology of Ethnocentrism: Evolutionary Dimensions of Xenophobia, Discrimination, Racism and Nationalism.* Edited by V. Reynolds, Vincent S. Falger, and Ian Vine. Athens: University of Georgia Press, 1987.

knows he is French or a German a German. Nationalism, in human terms, is almost always associated with war.* Not only are animals not ever at war with their own species (ants are, I suppose, but the warfare of ants is still little understood at anything like the psychological level), they are not ever at war with any other species, either. Humans are not only at war with one another, they are at war with other species, constantly (whales, for example), as demonstrated by the sad examples of species hunted to extinction. Hatred is not always the ultimate cause. Greed, stupidity, and ignorance bear their share of the blame.

In her brilliant book *Blood Rites,* Barbara Ehrenreich points out that predatory animals (eagles, hawks, lions, bears) play a major role in the flags and other symbols of countries. But not one of these animals ever wages war, nor does anything in their behavior resemble human warfare. As just explained, they are predators for a single reason: to eat. If they are not hungry, they do not hunt. Only rarely will any of these animals prey on one another. Thus, the use of these animal symbols is a result of misunderstanding.

Why is it that when we think we have discovered a human society free of aggression, or at least free of warfare, we make a tremendous fuss over it? We are immediately reminded that such peaceful coexistence is not beyond our capacity after all,

---

* "From the very beginning," the military historian Michael Howard has written, "the principle of nationalism was almost indissolubly linked, both in theory and practice, with the idea of war." Quoted by Barbara Ehrenreich, *Blood Rites: Origins and History of the Passions of War.* N.Y.: Henry Holt & Co., 1997, p. 196.

and we are admonished to learn what enabled this particular society to achieve something we thought beyond our species in general. Even though the vast majority of animal societies are in fact free of the kind of hatred found in human societies, books that tell us about the lack of aggression in animal societies, about cooperation, friendships, and helpfulness, are few and far between, and even more scarce are books dealing with altruism and compassion in animal societies. On the contrary, when we do turn to animal societies, we are reminded of their capacity for aggression, for fighting (think of the popularity of books with such titles as *Animals Harmful to Man* or simply *Aggression*). It is as if we felt that conceding any of these qualities of peacefulness to animals would be an assault on human dignity and even if true would best be passed over in humiliated silence.

Small children remind me of animals in their ability to *feel* compassion without thinking about it. For me, the whole experiment I conducted bore fruit when our two-year-old son, Manu, and Leila were in a sushi shop and Manu asked: "What sushi this?" Leila answered: "[Cooked] chicken sushi." Manu looked startled and said: "Moa? Moana? Me not eat it!" How can a two-year-old child make the connection that eludes so many adults? George Bernard Shaw famously said that if slaughterhouses were made of glass, the whole world would be vegetarian. I am not so sure. But would any of us eat a plate of meat if it contained the bodies of animals we had known personally, with whose life histories, eccentricities, and personalities we were intimately acquainted? If we knew them as *friends?* I think that is the secret to caring deeply for any animal: It is not merely knowledge, it is not merely seeing what happens to them, it is *knowing* them as people like us. For they are more like us than not. Even chickens. Even rats. After all, as I said earlier, isn't that the whole point of conducting experiments on rats? That their physiology, even their central nervous system, is so similar to ours that we can learn about ourselves from them? If they weren't like us, there would be no point in the experiment.

———————

PERHAPS IT IS possible for humans to change directions, to look at animals not as competitors or as yet another race to colonize, but as models for achieving something that has eluded humans for their entire evolutionary history. If animals can learn to live with other species in peace, and sometimes even in friendship, is it not possible that observing this extraordinary ability may yet act as a catalyst for us? Is it not possible that harmony among nations need be not a mere fantasy, but something we can learn from observing the achievements of these so-called lesser species? All that is lacking are the will and the humility.

Acknowledgments

As USUAL, my first and greatest debt goes to Nancy Miller, who is once again practically my co-writer. Happy the author who has such a friend and editor! Her assistants, Deirdre Lanning and Matt Kellogg, have been wonderful: helpful, cheerful, and efficient.

My wife, Leila, to whom I dedicate this book, accepted with empathy and an astonishing capacity for adaptation (even to chaos) a house full of animals. We share a great deal, but when it comes to love, Leila stands alone.

Robyn Haworth and Conny Ho were an enormous help from the very first day until the last. They have earned my eternal gratitude. Robyn's daughter Anneke and Rebecca Brown were exemplary assistants, helping in every aspect of the experiment.

I am indebted to Terese Storey who out of sheer pleasure in the project came once a week to play with the animals and talk with me about the project.

Gary Reese, the former head of Save Animals from Exploitation in Auckland, was often down at the beach talking with me about the project and simply enjoying the animals, all of whom seemed to have a special affection for this gentle man.

With patience, humor, and sometimes even delight, our neighbors Joan Chapple, Tony Watkins, and Corinna Koning put up with cats, rats, chickens, a dog, and a bunny invading their gardens and occasionally their homes.

Phil Evans was the deus ex machina who came from heaven at the end to rescue us all. Needless to say, my deepest thanks, and my most heartfelt gratitude, belong to seven persons: Mika, Tamaiti, Moa, Moana, Kia, Ora, and Hohepa.

ABOUT THE AUTHOR

JEFFREY MOUSSAIEFF MASSON, former psychoanalyst and previously the projects director of the Sigmund Freud Archives, is the bestselling author of more than a dozen books, including *Slipping into Paradise, The Pig Who Sang to the Moon, The Nine Emotional Lives of Cats, Dogs Never Lie About Love,* and *When Elephants Weep.* A longtime resident of Berkeley, California, he now lives in New Zealand with his wife, two sons, and several animal friends.

ABOUT THE TYPE

This book was set in Garamond, a typeface originally designed by the Parisian typecutter Claude Garamond (1480–1561). This version of Garamond was modeled on a 1592 specimen sheet from the Egenolff-Berner foundry, which was produced from types assumed to have been brought to Frankfurt by the punchcutter Jacques Sabon.

Claude Garamond's distinguished romans and italics first appeared in *Opera Ciceronis* in 1543–44. The Garamond types are clear, open, and elegant.